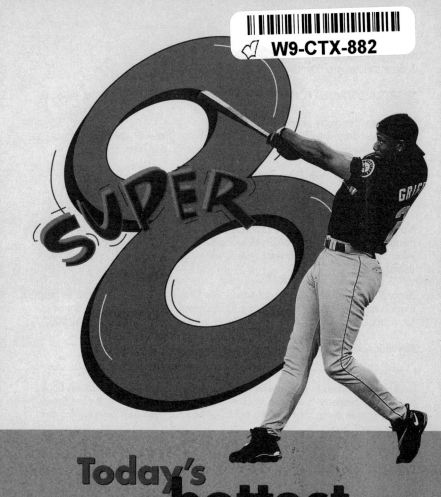

SUPER 8

Today's hottest sports stars

BY BOB KNOTTS

A SPORTS ILLUSTRATED FOR KIDS Book

Super 8 by Bob Knotts
A Sports Illustrated For Kids publication/November 1999

SPORTS ILLUSTRATED FOR KIDS and KiDS are registered trademarks of Time Inc.

Front-cover design by Sherry Sumerlin
Cover photographs by Barry Gossage/NBA Photos (Kobe Bryant), Tom DiPace
(Mark McGwire), J. Brett Whitesell/ISI (Mia Hamm), and George B. Fry III
(Terrell Davis)
Interior design by Emily Peterson Perez

Super 8 is published by Sports Illustrated For Kids, a division of Time Inc. Its trademark is registered in the U.S. Patent and Trademark Office and in other countries.
Sports Illustrated For Kids, 1271 Avenue of the Americas, New York, N.Y. 10020

For information, address: Sports Illustrated For Kids

ISBN 1-886749-68-X

Printed in the United States of America

10 9 8 7 6 5 4 3 2 1

Super 8 is a production of Sports Illustrated For Kids Books:
Cathrine Wolf, Assistant Managing Editor; Emily Peterson Perez, Art Director;
Amy Lennard Goehner and Margaret Sieck (Project Editor), Senior Editors;
Sherie Holder, Associate Editor; Nina Gaskin, Designer; Kathleen Fieffe, Reporter;
Robert J. Rohr, Copy Editor; Erin Tricarico, Photo Researcher; Ron Beuzenburg,
Production Manager

contents

dedication

To my wife, Jill; to my parents, Bill and
Jeanette; and to my editor, Margaret.
Thank you!

— B.K.

iNTRODUCTiON

Every day, something amazing happens in the world of sports. A baseball slugger slams an astounding home run. Or a football quarterback throws a game-winning, last-second touchdown pass. At any time, there's always something and someone to cheer about!

So, how can anyone choose the eight absolute hottest athletes in the world? Easy. We let kids help us figure that out. We looked at the readers' polls conducted by SPORTS ILLUSTRATED FOR KIDS magazine and other research we've done with kids around the country. We found the athletes who aren't just the hottest ones today but who are going to *stay* hot. *Super 8: Today's Hottest Sports Stars* identifies those athletes and tells their stories.

From the world of pro football, we have running back Terrell Davis of the Denver Broncos and quarterback Brett Favre of the Green Bay Packers. Los Angeles Laker Kobe Bryant and San Antonio Spur Tim Duncan are our pro basketball big shots, and Mia Hamm comes from the U.S. Women's Soccer Team. Baseball blasters Ken Griffey, Junior, of the Seattle Mariners, Mark McGwire of the St. Louis Cardinals, and Sammy Sosa of the Chicago Cubs round out the group.

All eight athletes are champions. Many have overcome great obstacles along the path to fame. All of them have become examples to kids who want to be like them. These players are great. They are the *Super 8!*

SUPER 8 TERRELL DAVIS

Hard work transformed this hard-luck kid into a winner

Yes, he certainly has the moves today. That running back is twirling like some crazy dancer out there on the football field. The quarterback hands him the ball, and suddenly, the huge, quick defensive players who are trying to stop him look silly, falling all over themselves and grabbing the air. Trying to stop Terrell Davis of the Denver Broncos is like trying to grab a greased pig.

This is the biggest game of the 1998 season — Super Bowl XXXIII. The Denver Broncos are playing the Atlanta Falcons for the NFL championship. Millions of fans around the world are watching on TV. But the pressure doesn't bother Terrell. He's a clutch player.

Just one year earlier, Terrell won the Super Bowl MVP award and helped Denver take the NFL title from the Green Bay Packers, 31–24. He did some amazing things that day. One of the most astonishing was his quick recovery during the game from a terrible migraine headache. Terrell came back after halftime and showed the Packers no mercy. And here he is, one year later, doing it all over again to another Super Bowl opponent. He keeps burning the Atlanta defense, over and over.

The Broncos are setting up now on offense behind their great quarterback, John Elway. John shouts out the count, takes the snap, and drops back as if he were going to pass. Instead, he gives the ball to Terrell once more. The running back starts using his tricks, putting those famous moves on the Falcons. His strong legs chug up and down like the pistons of an engine. He spins and darts upfield, dipping a shoulder, breaking tackles right and left. Fifteen yards later, the outmatched Atlanta defense drags him down.

But this was no ordinary run. This was a small piece of National Football League history. With that carry, Terrell has rushed for more than 100 yards. That means he has just broken the all-time record for most 100-yard games in a row during post-season play — seven of them! He also tied his own record of fourteen 100-yard efforts in one season (regular season and post-season), a record he shares with All-Pro running back Barry Sanders.

Not Always a Sports Star

You can almost tell what a great football player Terrell is just by watching him walk along the sideline. It is obvious that he's a natural athlete. He looks as if he started playing football soon after he started to walk! You feel sure this is a guy who has been a sports star all his life, from elementary school to the pros. He probably always knew he'd become one of the best in the NFL — and probably everybody who saw him play knew, too. That's the way things *look* now anyway. But it's *not* so.

The truth is that life hasn't been easy for Terrell. Even football wasn't always easy. He grew up in a rough neighborhood, a place filled with gangs, guns, and drugs. Violence was part of his home life for a long time. Terrell did not play high school football until his junior year. He was not a standout player in college. Pro teams weren't interested in signing him to a contract. After he was drafted, he struggled like mad just to make it onto the Broncos roster.

Terrell has established himself as one of the top running backs in football. He became rich and famous by excelling in a sport that he loves. But he remembers when things weren't so good for him, a time when things weren't good at all.

Tough Times at Home

Terrell was born on October 28, 1972, in San Diego, California. He grew up there in a little home on Florence Street. He was the youngest of six boys. The others were Joe Junior, James, Reggie, Bobby, and Terry. The Davis family was poor. But poverty wasn't the only problem young Terrell faced. He had health troubles, too. At only 7 years of age, he began to suffer from migraine headaches. Migraines are painful and usually strike without warning.

Terrell's father, Joe Davis, could also strike without warning. He was known to beat his boys. This was a violent man who told himself he was making his boys tough by hurting them. He was known to beat them with an electrical cord. He would drink too much and take drugs, and the boys never

TERRELL DAVIS

TERRELL TIDBITS

BIRTH DATE: October 28, 1972

HEIGHT: 5' 11"   **WEIGHT:** 210 pounds

HOME: Aurora, Colorado

COLLEGE MAJOR: Consumer economics

MULTI-PURPOSE MAN: Played six different positions in high school

LITTLE KNOWN HIGH SCHOOL FACT: Lettered in track

HE'S A WRITER: Co-author of his autobiography — *TD: Dreams in Motion*

FAVORITE ACTIVITY (OTHER THAN PLAYING FOOTBALL): Playing TV video games

FAVORITE VIDEO GAME: Madden Football '99

knew how he would act when he stumbled in the door at night. Terrell hated him for his behavior.

It wasn't bad *all* the time, of course. Sometimes Mr. Davis was fun to be around. He bought gifts, told jokes, sang along to songs by the Temptations. But the boys knew his violent side was never far away.

Terrell's mom, Kateree, was very different from his dad. Kateree took college courses *and* worked full-time. She cooked, cleaned, and raised her family. She worried a lot about her sons, too. Kateree knew they lived in a bad neighborhood, a place where many kids got into serious trouble.

"The only one I didn't worry about was Terrell," she said.

"The other boys . . . when they went out the door, I always wondered if they would come back. I never felt that way about Terrell. He always had a maturity about him."

Terrell was a good student in school. He also worked hard, rising early in the morning to deliver newspapers. And he was a fine running back in Pop Warner football. But then, when Terrell was 14, his father grew very ill with a disease called lupus. It wasn't long before Joe Davis died. He was only 42 years old.

The death changed everyone in the family, including Terrell. He had hated his father's meanness, yet he had loved his father, too. Mr. Davis had been tough and had helped keep Terrell in line. Without him, Terrell lost some of the direction in his life. Now he entered Morse High School and goofed off. He ignored teachers and skipped classes. He didn't

The Name Game

Where did Terrell get his name? From a singer. A rhythm-and-blues artist named Tammy Terrell recorded a song with Marvin Gaye, a famous singer in the 1970's. Their duet had a line that went "Ain't nothing like the real thing, baby." Terrell's mother liked the song and picked Tammy's last name for youngest son.

study anymore. He didn't even play football. "My teachers couldn't stand me," Terrell recalled. "I can't blame them."

His brothers got into far worse trouble. Terry was ordered to serve 245 days in a work camp for punching a teacher. Bobby was convicted of two serious crimes and sentenced to 11 years in prison.

Terrell started to worry about himself. Was he going to ruin his life? Was he going to wind up like his brothers? No, he didn't want that. So Terrell transferred to a different high school, where he could start over. He went to summer school to improve his grades, studied hard — and played football again. He began to turn things around.

Lincoln Prep High School already had a running back when Terrell arrived. No problem. Terrell was happy to play kicker and nose guard on defense.

"I liked the teachers [at Lincoln]," Terrell said. "I got involved in extracurricular activities. I wrestled. I ran track."

In his senior year, Terrell finally got to carry the football for Lincoln. Terrell's performance was good — not great. He chalked up 700 yards as a running back, and his team made the city playoffs. He didn't get college scholarship offers, as he had hoped to get. The future looked uncertain again.

Terrell's brother Reggie helped Terrell finally land a football scholarship at Long Beach State. But Terrell didn't play much. After two years, Long Beach dropped its football program. The biggest thing in his college life was suddenly gone. Now what? Terrell knew he would have to transfer to another school.

A recruiting trip convinced Terrell that the University of

Georgia was the best place to go. But he ended up having a tough time at Georgia. Though he rushed for 824 yards as a junior, he ran for only 445 yards in his senior year.

The reasons Terrell didn't perform well are complex. For one thing, he didn't get along with his coach, Ray Goff. Another thing was that, according to Terrell, Coach Goff forced Terrell to play even though he had a hamstring injury. Terrell then hurt his hamstring *more* seriously and missed three games his senior year. His injury helped to earn him an unfair reputation as a player who was easily injured. All this could not have happened at a worse time because it was Terrell's senior year, right before the NFL draft.

A Disappointing Draft

As difficult as it is to believe now, the NFL had little interest in Terrell. He was the 196th player picked during the 1995 draft! Twenty running backs were chosen before the Denver Broncos selected him. When training camp began, he was listed last on the Broncos' depth chart (a ranking of players at each position). After that, Terrell's goal was just to make the practice squad!

Everyone felt certain this kid was nothing more than "camp meat." That's what players call athletes who attend training camp but have almost no chance to make the team. Again, hard work paid off for Terrell. He played as if his life depended on it — and in a way, it did. He was determined to prove he belonged in the NFL.

Terrell showed serious running talent in the pre-season. He also blocked hard, caught tough passes, even made

12

TERRELL DAVIS

fierce tackles. In one exhibition game, against the San Francisco 49ers, the coach put him on special teams to cover a Denver kickoff. Terrell dodged one blocker and hammered the ballcarrier for the tackle. "Terrell knocked the guy back fifteen feet," remembered Reggie Rivers, a Bronco running back. "It was incredible."

Coaches liked what they saw. "I tell my players, 'You're either coachable or you're a coach-killer,'" Bobby Turner, Denver running-back coach, explained. "You tell Terrell something once, he gets it. Tell him twice, he owns it. He's coachable."

Terrell made the team. But he couldn't take it easy. He knew it was important to show everyone his best stuff in that first year. Terrell did that in a big way. In only his third pro game, he scored three touchdowns against the Washington Redskins! For the season, he rushed for 1,117 yards and seven touchdowns and caught 49 passes for 367 yards. When the year was over, Terrell came in second in the voting for the NFL Offensive Rookie of the Year award.

Combining Power and Speed

What makes Terrell such a great running back is his unusual combination of power and speed. He can also cut and dodge well to avoid tacklers and is known for being able to adjust to different defenses easily. He can move outside if he needs to and doesn't just take the ball up the middle. "There's not an area in his game that isn't strong," said Denver coach Mike Shanahan.

The next season was even better. In 1996, Terrell led the

American Football Conference with 1,538 running yards. He rushed for 100 or more yards in five of the first six games. And he did it while struggling with migraines in some games.

In the 1997 season, Terrell continued to improve. He had 1,750 yards, with 15 rushing touchdowns and 42 pass receptions. He won the rushing title in the AFC for the second straight season and ran for more first downs than anyone in the entire NFL. In the post-season, Terrell carried the ball for 581 yards and eight TDs in four games.

But Terrell, headaches and all, saved his best for the Super Bowl. There is never a good time to have a migraine headache. Many people who suffer from them must stay in bed until the symptoms pass. But Terrell had one while playing in his first Super Bowl, in January 1998!

Super Bowl XXXII took place in San Diego — Terrell's hometown. His family was in the middle of the massive crowd at the stadium. Terrell's mom said later that the lights and noise and all the emotion were almost too much for her to bear that day. The fans were pumped for a great game. The Green Bay Packers, Denver's opponent, were the reigning world champs. They had a great quarterback, Brett Favre (see page 17). Many people expected the Packers to win the Super Bowl for the second year in a row. They just might have done it too, if not for Terrell.

The game seemed up for grabs after Terrell took a hard hit to the head in the first quarter. He started to feel dizzy and sick to his stomach. He blacked out for several seconds. When Terrell woke up, his vision was a mess: He saw three of everything! "I couldn't see," he said. "I knew it was the

TERRELL DAVIS

Super Bowl!'" Terrell spent the entire second quarter taking medication and oxygen treatments.

After halftime, though, Terrell re-entered the big game. "My vision was back, and I knew I was going to be okay," he recalled. He was a lot more than just okay. Though he

Amazing Mom

Kateree Davis, Terrell's mother, showed in many ways over the years that she was a champion, too. Yes, it's tough to play NFL football. But it's even tougher to raise a large, poor family in a violent neighborhood. Kateree was just 16 when she married. By the time she was 23, she was pregnant with Terrell, her sixth son. She dropped out of high school. But Kateree was determined and strong. She worked until midnight, then studied, cooked meals, cleaned the house, and got the kids ready for school. After graduating from college, she worked double shifts. "I never saw anyone with as much energy as my mother," Terrell said. No wonder Terrell grew up to be such a hard worker!

he recalled. He was a lot more than just okay. Though he fumbled on his first carry, Terrell rushed for 93 yards and two touchdowns in the final 30 minutes. His performance helped Denver to control the ball and the game clock. When the game was over, Denver had won, 31–24.

"I think the Packers have migraines now," Terrell said afterward. He ended up with 157 yards for the day — and the Super Bowl Most Valuable Player award.

The next season, Terrell was at it again. He won his first NFL rushing title with 2,008 yards and 21 TDs. He was only the fourth NFL player ever to run for more than 2,000 yards in a single season! He was picked as Most Valuable Player and Offensive Player of the Year by the Associated Press. He was selected to start in his third straight Pro Bowl game.

Terrell and the Broncos topped off the 1998 season with another Super Bowl victory. The halfback no one in the NFL really wanted had earned his second Super Bowl ring in only four seasons.

Never Giving Up

Terrell had turned his life around. Things were good. He bought a beautiful home and built his mother a house nearby. But in the fourth game of the 1999 season, Terrell damaged his knee and was out for the season. Still, almost everyone in the country knew Terrell's name and what he could do with a football.

No one expected this kid from a bad neighborhood to do so well. Few would have cared if he had quit. But he didn't quit. Terrell worked hard and never gave up on himself.

SUPER 8 BRETT FAVRE

This quarterback strong-armed his way into the NFL's top ranks

Brett Favre is one of the most dangerous men in the National Football League. The Green Bay Packer quarterback can cut through opposing players faster than a hot knife slices butter. He stands at the line of scrimmage looking over the defense. He stands there, shouting signals, changing plays instantly, if that's what is needed. Once the ball is in his hands, Brett can throw from the pocket or while he's running. Most of the time, Brett's passes are perfect bullets, and often, they go for big touchdowns.

Many of these skills were seen during Super Bowl XXXI, in January 1997. The Packers were playing the New England Patriots. Early in the second quarter, Brett noticed the Patriot defense lining up for man-to-man coverage of Green Bay's three wide receivers. So Brett changed the play on the spot by calling an audible — a coded signal that changes a play just before the ball is snapped. The change allowed Brett to quickly hit his receiver, Antonio Freeman. Touchdown! And what a touchdown. The scoring play was 81 yards long, and

17

it was the longest touchdown from scrimmage in Super Bowl history! The Packers went on to win the game, 35–21.

Brett is a dangerous man on a football field — and he's not just dangerous to opponents. "He once broke my finger on a pass," recalled Mark Chmura, a Packer tight end. "Sometimes Brett has no idea how hard he throws. Your hands have to be out and ready."

There also have been times when Brett was more dangerous off the gridiron than on it — dangerous to himself. He drank too much alcohol. He became addicted to pain-killing pills that threatened to end his career . . . and maybe his life. Alcohol and drugs had become very serious problems.

But Brett fought hard against his troubles off the field and won, just as he has always fought hard on the field. Brett has proven again and again that he's a true champion. Those qualities helped Brett lead the Packers to two Super Bowls and become the first player to win three straight NFL Most Valuable Player awards.

"Brett is pure magic," Green Bay fullback William Henderson says. "When he's under pressure, he makes miracles happen."

By the Bayou

The tiny Mississippi town of Kiln [pronounced kill] is Brett Lorenzo Favre's hometown. When Brett was a kid, in the 1970's, Kiln had only 800 resident. Brett lived outside of town, in the country. That country upbringing is still with him. Once, wide receiver Andre Rison called him a hillbilly. Brett thanked him. "Because I am," Brett said.

BRETT FAVRE

Kiln sits next to a body of water called Rotten Bayou. Young Brett often skipped rocks across the bayou's alligator-infested water. The Favre family's dogs also played near the water. Three of them got a little too close: Alligators ate them!

Brett was like most boys. For example, he didn't like cleaning his room. He even slept on top of his sheets so that he didn't have to make the bed in the morning. He loved sports. His idols growing up were two quarterbacks for teams in the South: Roger Staubach of the Dallas Cowboys and Archie Manning of the New Orleans Saints. He dreamed of becoming a great NFL passer, just as they were.

An All-around Athlete

Brett soon proved to be a talented all-around athlete. At Hancock North Central High School, in Kiln, he earned a varsity letter every year in baseball and led his team in batting every season. He also earned three varsity letters for playing on the high school football team, which was coached by his father, Irvin. Brett could do many different things on the football field. At various times, he played quarterback, strong safety, punter, and placekicker. After his senior season, he was named to play on the Mississippi high school all-star team.

Brett wasn't the only talented athlete in his family. His dad had pitched for the University of Southern Mississippi varsity baseball team. Two of Brett's brothers played college football. Scott, who is one year older, was a quarterback at Mississippi State University. Jeff, four years younger, was a free safety for Southern Mississippi. Brett's sister, Brandi, excelled in another area: She earned the title of Miss Teen Mississippi.

In 1987, Brett entered the University of Southern Mississippi, the same college his dad attended. In only the third game of his freshman year, Brett became the football team's starting quarterback! In his college career, he set school records for the most touchdowns, completions, and passing yards, and for the highest passing percentage. Brett had an interception ratio of 1.57 (the number of interceptions per passes thrown). It was best among the 50 top-ranked college quarterbacks in the United States.

But on July 14, 1990, just before Brett's senior year, he was in a terrible car crash. He suffered a concussion, cuts, bruises, and a cracked vertebra. Three weeks later, doctors discovered that he had serious internal injuries, as well. Surgeons had to remove 30 inches of his intestines.

But Brett is tough. His recovery was surprisingly quick. He was back as starting quarterback only one month after the accident. He led his team to an upset over Alabama in his first game back, on September 8, 1990.

At the end of his senior year, Brett was named MVP of the 1990 All-American Bowl, a post-season bowl game. NFL scouts were impressed with his daring on the field and his missile-fast passes. After a scouting trip to watch Brett, a top official with one pro team said, "I just saw the NFL's next great quarterback."

Brett's pro career began soon afterward, but it wasn't so great. In April 1991, he was selected by the Atlanta Falcons in the second round of the NFL draft. In his first season, he

BRETT FAVRE

BRETT'S BIO

BIRTH DATE: October 10, 1969
HEIGHT: 6' 2"   **WEIGHT:** 220 pounds
HOMES: Hattiesburg, Mississippi, and Green Bay, Wisconsin
COLLEGE MAJOR: Special Education
FAVORITE SPORTS TO PLAY (OTHER THAN FOOTBALL): Basketball, golf, and fishing
FAVORITE CANDY BAR: Brett Favre MVP Bar
FAVORITE DESSERT: Cookies-and-cream ice cream

was on the active roster (meaning he was eligible to play) for just three games. He played in two of them and attempted five passes without completing even one. Not the best start for an NFL quarterback!

Brett now admits that he messed things up in his early days as a pro. For one thing, he drank too much. He also didn't take the time to learn Atlanta's plays because, as a rookie, he thought he had little hope of playing. He didn't always show up when he was supposed to for team activities. Head Coach Jerry Glanville didn't like Brett's attitude.

One time, Coach Glanville fined Brett $1,500 for showing up late to a team photo session. "I got trapped behind a car wreck," Brett explained. The coach didn't buy this excuse. "Boy, you *are* a car wreck," he replied.

21

The next spring, Atlanta traded Brett to Green Bay for a first-round draft pick. Brett had not shown the Falcons much. They had no reason to think he would have a great career. Over the winter, Brett had gained weight. He was out of shape. His future didn't look good.

Throwing Wild

But Packer head coach Mike Holmgren recognized Brett's potential. Soon, the young passer got a chance to show what he could do. In the first quarter of the third game of the 1992 season, Packer starting quarterback Don Majkowski was injured. The Packers needed someone to replace him. Coach Holmgren turned to Brett, and he came through dramatically! With just 13 seconds left, Brett launched a 35-yard touchdown pass to defeat the Cincinnati Bengals, 24–23.

Several years later, Brett admitted that he was lucky that first day. He said his performance was wild. "I should have thrown six or seven interceptions," Brett told *Sports Illustrated*. "I was throwing darts off guys' helmets, trying to throw the ball through people. I still didn't know the offense at all."

This had been a problem for Brett in Atlanta when he started out, and it remained a problem for him for a long time afterward: He didn't learn the complicated offenses used in the NFL. But somehow, he still was able to play well enough to remain the Packer starter. In fact, he made the Pro Bowl in 1992 and 1993! But Brett often ignored Green Bay's system. He was scrambling and throwing risky passes whenever plays didn't go smoothly. His frustrated

BRETT FAVRE

coach often pleaded with him: "Let the system work for you!"

By early in the 1994 season, the Packer coaches were tired of Brett's inconsistency. A talented back-up quarterback, Mark Brunell, sat in the wings, waiting for his chance. Coach Holmgren asked each of his assistants who he believed should start as the Packers' passer. Mark got more votes than Brett.

But Coach Holmgren wasn't so sure. He thought for a while before reaching his decision. He chose Brett. Coach Holmgren could tell how talented Brett was. It troubled the coach that Brett was wasting all that talent. He called Brett into his office

"It's just you and me, buddy," Mr. Holmgren told him. "We're joined at the hip. Either we're going to the Super Bowl together or we're going down together."

A Changed Man

Brett couldn't believe it. He had been sure that the coach was ready to bench him. This great vote of confidence was exactly what Brett needed. "Just hearing Mike say that saved me," he recalled later.

Brett was a new quarterback after that meeting with Coach Holmgren. He started using the Packer system instead of just making it up as he went along. He fired 24 touchdown passes over the rest of the season, with only seven interceptions. He also came in second in the MVP balloting, behind Steve Young of the San Francisco 49ers.

Brett's real glory years began in 1995. During that season, he led the Packers to the NFC championship game and was named the NFL's Most Valuable Player. He threw 38

A Giving Guy

In 1996, Brett started the Brett Favre Forward Foundation, which raises hundreds of thousands of dollars for charities through an annual golf tournament.

Brett also has brought in lots of cash for the Boys & Girls Club of Green Bay. How? He donates $150 for each TD he scores by passing or rushing. Even better, he has arranged for several corporations to match his donations. Altogether, these contributions totaled $164,000 for the Boys & Girls Club in 1998 alone!

touchdown passes. Only one NFL quarterback had ever thrown more in a single season. (It was Dan Marino of the Miami Dolphins, and he did it twice — throwing 48 touchdown passes in 1984 and 44 in 1986.) Brett also was chosen as starting quarterback in the Pro Bowl.

But Brett had a huge problem in his personal life by this time. He had become addicted to a painkiller called Vicodin. Over the years, he had suffered dozens of injuries playing football. He had had some major operations, but he didn't want to stop playing. So, he was given prescriptions for the pills to dull his pain.

BRETT FAVRE

But after awhile, he wasn't taking the pills just to kill the pain. Brett started to think that Vicodin actually sharpened his quarterback talents! He took more of the pills than he should have and at times when he really didn't need them. This was a big mistake. In February 1996, while he was in the hospital for ankle surgery, Brett experienced a seizure. His body shook uncontrollably as his arms, legs, and head flailed wildly. It was scary.

Soon, Brett learned that Vicodin might well have caused the seizure. That made him realize that he had a terrible addiction. For help, he entered a special rehabilitation clinic for 45 days. He held a press conference before he entered the clinic and told the world about his problem. He also assured everyone that his addiction to pills was over for good.

Brett was drug-free by the start of the 1996 season, and he was playing better than ever. He had his best season yet! He connected for 39 touchdown passes. He rushed for 136 yards and two more touchdowns! Brett was a Pro Bowl starter again and took home his second straight MVP award.

It was a great season for Green Bay, too. The Packers had once been a mighty football dynasty. They won Super Bowl I and Super Bowl II in 1967 and 1968. But 28 years went by without another NFL championship. Brett's brilliant quarterbacking helped end that drought at last.

Super Bowl XXXI (for the 1996 season) was played in New Orleans, a Louisiana city only about one hour from Brett's hometown. Many family members and friends planned to be at the Superdome, where the Packers would meet the New England Patriots. Brett was very excited. But then he came down with a flu bug in the days leading up to the game and could hardly drag himself out of bed. He could only practice a short time.

"I was worried," Brett said. "I waited my whole life to play in [the Super Bowl], and now I wasn't going to be healthy."

On Super Bowl Sunday, Brett woke up feeling ready to take on the Patriots. He was still sick, but he felt he could play. And play he did! He made two long touchdown passes, to Andre Rison and Antonio Freeman. He scored another TD himself by barreling in from the two-yard line. Brett helped the Packers beat the Patriots, 35–21.

"It would be great to win anywhere," a grinning Brett told reporters after the game. "But being so close to home . . . I don't believe this could be better." Packer fans were delighted, too: They finally had their third championship!

The 1997 season was another great one for Brett. He led the NFL in touchdown passes, with 35, and became the first NFL quarterback to throw 30 or more TDs in four straight seasons. Here's another impressive stat: Brett connected for more touchdown passes in a four-season span than anyone in NFL history except the Dolphins' Dan Marino.

Most important of all, Brett led the Packers back to the Super Bowl, in January 1998. This time, they ran into super-star John Elway and a determined Denver Bronco team and lost, 31–24. But Brett stung the Broncos for three TDs and 256 yards. He shared regular-season MVP honors with Barry Sanders, the great Detroit Lion running back.

The 1998 season turned into something of a disappoint-ment for Brett. After three outstanding seasons and two trips

BRETT FAVRE

Brett Goes Hollywood

Brett is a good-looking guy and he isn't exactly camera shy. He has acted in a major Hollywood movie! Brett made a brief appearance near the end of the 1998 film *There's Something About Mary*. The movie starred actress Cameron Diaz as Mary. The movie was a big success. In 1997, Brett appeared in *Reggie's Prayer,* a film put together by his former Green Bay teammate Reggie White. Brett has also been a guest on many national TV shows, including "The Tonight Show with Jay Leno" and "The Late Show with David Letterman."

It makes you wonder if Brett is gunning for a career in front of the camera after he's thrown his last touchdown bomb!

to the Super Bowl, he and the Packers just didn't quite have the same success. The team was upset by the San Francisco 49ers, 30–27, during the first round of the playoffs in the NFC. During the regular season, Brett threw more interceptions than he had since 1993 — 23 of them.

Brett began to realize that he couldn't be young and great

forever. In May 1999, Brett told *Sports Illustrated* that he was concerned about his future. "I'll be thirty this year, and I don't want to be the forgotten man," he said.

Brett would be pretty hard to forget! For one thing, he put up some great numbers during the 1998 season. He completed 347 passes for 4,212 yards and 31 TDs. He started all 16 regular-season games for the sixth straight year!

Most important, though, Brett had left some bad habits behind and found new meaning in his world. Instead of going out a lot, partying and drinking too much, he had become a family man. "I've lived a fun, hard life," Brett said. "But fun now is watching [my daughter] Brittany play softball. Fun is having rookies in the weight room look at me as an example of what they want to be. I'm done with alcohol."

In July 1999, Brett's wife, Deanna, gave birth to another daughter, Breleigh Ann. "He was pretty excited," Brett's mother told reporters. " 'He just kept smiling and saying, "She's daddy's little girl.' "

A Role Model At Last

Brett Favre has come a long way. He now understands his responsibilities to himself, to his family, to his team — and to others. "I'm getting a lot of letters from parents and teachers telling me I'm a role model, which is something I never thought I'd be," Brett told *Time* magazine. "And some people are writing to tell me I've given them the courage to face their own problems. That's not why I stopped [drinking], to be an inspiration. But if I help people while I'm helping myself, that's okay."

SUPER 8 KOBE BRYANT

Young and talented, this guard made a great leap to the NBA

The game is on the line, and the Los Angeles Lakers need help. It's January 19, 1998. The Lakers are playing the Orlando Magic in L.A.'s Great Western Forum. With just a little time left, the Lakers lead by only 1 point. The Lakers could use some anti-Magic magic to clinch the victory.

Laker forward Robert Horry tries to make it happen. He stands at the free throw line, concentrating hard before he arcs his shot toward the backboard. He misses. He shoots again. The ball bounces off, and it looks like no score for the Lakers. *Wait!* The play isn't over! Twisting his body like a cat, guard Kobe Bryant instantly slips in front of Danny Schayes of the Magic. Kobe is playing in only his second NBA season, but he reaches up, as if he had been doing this forever, and taps the ball lightly. Two points! Kobe's dazzling move puts the Lakers up by three!

It did not last. With 22 seconds left, two Orlando free throws make the score 89–88. Laker guard Nick Van Exel is fouled immediately, but makes only one free throw. The score is now 90–88. With the clock running down, Magic forward Horace Grant is fouled. As the opposing teams line up for the foul shots, the Magic's Derek Harper looks at Kobe and lays some trash talk on the 19-year-old kid. "Let a veteran show you how to knock down a couple of free throws," Derek razzes.

Talk is cheap, though. Horace makes one shot and then misses the next. Derek and his teammates are scrambling to win the game. L.A. still leads, 90–89. They are forced to commit a quick foul to stop the clock. Worse yet: They have no choice except to foul Kobe!

"Let a young fella show you how to do it," Kobe teases back as he takes the ball to the free throw line. There are just 7.7 seconds left to play in the game as Kobe gazes at the basket. Coolly and cleanly, he sinks first one shot and then the second to ice the 92–89 victory for Los Angeles. Once again, the cool kid has shown the tough veterans just what he can do with a basketball in his hands.

Can-Do Kobe

Kobe Bryant is truly an amazing young player. How many athletes — in any sport — go straight from high school to the big time, as he did? How many are almost instantly compared to the greatest star their sport has ever known? How many can withstand the pressure that comes along with being "the next Michael Jordan" and still deliver when it counts? Kobe can.

Game after game since joining the NBA, in 1996, Kobe

KOBE BRYANT

has proved that his talent is the real thing. By his third season (1998-99), he was regarded as one of the best players in the league — although he was only 20! Listen to one of his teammates: "Hey, next time he does something . . . take your eyes off Kobe, if you can, and look at the Laker bench," suggests Robert Horry. "We're over there going, 'Oh-hhh!' just like everybody else. The stuff he does is incredible."

A European Education

Kobe was born to shoot a basketball. His father, Joe "Jelly Bean" Bryant, played in the NBA for eight years. Joe specialized in defense, coming off the bench to guard the opposing team's best players. He played for several teams but he started out with the Philadelphia 76ers. He was part of the Philly team that made it all the way to the 1977 NBA Finals.

Kobe was born a year later, on August 23, 1978, in Philadelphia, Pennsylvania. He is the youngest child and the only son in the family. He has two older sisters, Sharia and Shaya. His mother's name is Pamela. After Joe's NBA career ended, in 1984, the Bryants packed up for a true adventure. They moved to Rieti, Italy, so that Joe could continue playing pro basketball. This turned out to be a very important event in Kobe's life.

Kobe started school in Europe. He was 6 years old, entering the first grade. His sisters were entering second and third grades. None of the Bryant children spoke Italian, so they had to work like crazy just to get their education.

"My two sisters and I got together after school to teach

one another the words we had learned," Kobe recalled. "I was able to speak Italian pretty well within a few months." Kobe remembers eating lots of pasta and walking through the Alps mountains with his family on Saturdays.

The Bryants lived in Italy for eight years, but it wasn't all lasagna and Alps! Because he was the son of a basketball player, Kobe learned to play basketball, too — even though soccer was the most popular sport for Italian kids. "After school, I would be the only guy on the basketball court, working on my moves," Kobe said.

Learning By Watching

Kobe was able to do some things that he would not have done had he lived in the United States. Kobe often practiced beside his father's team after school. He even shot baskets during halftime at the team's games. The crowd cheered him on, and Kobe loved it.

Then there were the videotapes. Kobe's grandparents back in the U.S. taped the best NBA games and mailed off the videos every couple of days. Kobe and his dad watched them together as Dad explained what was happening on the court and why it was happening. Kobe replayed those tapes many times, memorizing the plays and learning from the stars of the NBA. Kobe and his dad especially enjoyed videos of the Laker games. They watched videos of about 40 Los Angeles games a year. Kobe was already a Laker fan. He even had worn a small Laker team jacket as a baby!

Kobe says those videotapes helped him learn to play the way he does today. "My baseline jumper, I got it from [Hall of Fame guard] Oscar Robertson," he told *Sports Illustrated*. "Oscar liked to use his size against smaller players. That's what I try to do." Kobe said his fallaway jump shot came from copying center Hakeem Olajuwon of the Houston Rockets. He learned from even older tapes of New York Knick Earl "the Pearl" Monroe how to "shake one way, then go back the other way." Earl was a brilliant ball handler.

In 1992, the Bryants returned to the United States and lived in Philadelphia. Kobe was 14. He soon joined a summer basketball league in Philadelphia. On his league application, Kobe wrote that his future career would be in the NBA. A counselor scolded him for it. "The guy said NBA players are one in a million," he recalled. "I said, 'Man, look, I'm going to be that one in a million.'"

Player of the Year

The boy began proving his point before long. Kobe was the star at Lower Merion High School, in Ardmore, Pennsylvania. He was a starter as a freshman and every year after that. In his final three seasons, he helped the team to a 77–13 record! *USA Today* and *Parade* magazine picked Kobe as the National High School Player of the Year during his senior season.

Kobe was 6' 5" tall and averaged more than 30 points a game — thanks in part to some serious slam-dunking skills. Kobe also led his team to a state title during his senior season. He was awesome! He was so famous that when he announced that he wanted to take the singer Brandy to his prom, she accepted!

BOXFUL OF BRYANT

BIRTH DATE: August 23, 1978

HEIGHT: 6' 7"   **WEIGHT:** 210 pounds

HOME: Pacific Palisades, California

COLLEGE: None, but he has taken courses at the University of California at Los Angeles

FAVORITE SPORT TO PLAY (OTHER THAN BASKETBALL): Soccer

FAVORITE SPORT TO WATCH (OTHER THAN BASKETBALL): Tennis

FAVORITE FOODS: Lasagna and apple pie

FAVORITE ATHLETES: Football players Barry Sanders and Emmitt Smith

FAVORITE HOBBY: "Dancing. I love all types of dancing."

PLACE HE WOULD MOST LIKE TO VISIT: North Pole

After all this success, then what? Most high school stars go to college and hope to some day become a pro. Hardly anybody had gone straight to the pros. But Kobe wasn't anybody. Sure, he was a solid B student in school who could have gone to a good university and played in one of the best college basketball programs. But he didn't do that.

Instead, Kobe decided to join the world's best players . . . the National Basketball Association. It was quite a leap — from shooting against high school guys to taking on Michael

KOBE BRYANT

Jordan! But Kobe, his parents, and his coach all thought he could do it. And so did some NBA teams.

The Charlotte Hornets chose Kobe as the 13th overall pick in 1996, then traded him that same day to Los Angeles. The kid was going to play for the team he had always loved! He also was going to work for one of his idols: former Laker superstar Magic Johnson. Magic had retired as a player in 1991 and had become a Laker vice president.

"It's like God blessed that trade so that Kobe could come out here and be around a guy who can help him by sitting and watching him every night," Magic said. "I'm going to take care of him. But I'm also going to criticize him when he has to be criticized."

Kobe began to live his dream. He was playing for the Lakers — and Magic Johnson was watching *him* instead of the other way around. Kobe even got Magic's old locker!

Kobe's first season, 1996-97, was respectable for a rookie. He played in 71 games, starting six times, and averaging nearly 8 points per game. On January 28, 1997, in Dallas, Kobe became the youngest player ever to start an NBA game. After the season, he was selected for the NBA All-Rookie Second Team.

During the 1997-98 season, Kobe really began to show his talents. Though he started only once, he played in 79 games and established himself as the Lakers' valuable "sixth man." The sixth man is the first player to come off the bench to substitute for one of the starters. A good sixth man is as valuable as a starter. Kobe certainly was valuable to the Lakers. He scored in double-figures (10 or more points) in 65 games. One time he scored 27 points in less than 13 minutes!

In February 1998, Kobe became the youngest All-Star in NBA history. He started for the Western Conference at the age of 19 years 5 months 16 days. Kobe was hyped as Michael Jordan's big rival in that All-Star Game. A full-page newspaper ad pictured these two players alone, face to face. "I said, 'Cool,' " Kobe says. "It was like they were making it out to be some big one-on-one showdown."

Kobe responded well to the pressure. He scored 18 points, the highest individual total for the Western squad. Kobe also showed up on all the highlight tapes after making the most awesome play of the game: a behind the back dribble that ended with a breakaway slam dunk. Showtime!

The next season was delayed by the NBA lockout. Still, Kobe continued to improve. He played in all 50 of the team's games in the strike-shortened regular season. He averaged nearly 20 points per game and led the Lakers in scoring in 11 games. Once, he scored 38 points in a game — 33 of them in the second half! Kobe banged the boards too. He put together nine double-doubles for the year (scoring 10 or more points and grabbing 10 or more rebounds).

After the season, Kobe was named to the 1998-99 All-NBA Third Team. The comparisons with Michael Jordan kept coming. One of the comparisons came from a pretty good source — Phil Jackson, who had coached Michael with the Chicago Bulls. The Lakers hired Coach Jackson in June 1999 to run their team. Guess what he told reporters? He said that Kobe reminded him of Michael!

KOBE BRYANT

By then, Kobe was so well-known that he had his *own* line of sneakers — and they were selling well! He was making a lot of money from the Lakers and from endorsing other products. But all the fame and money didn't seem to go to Kobe's head. He still lived with his parents and sisters, in a house he bought. His mother cooked for him, but Kobe did his own laundry. When asked what he liked to do after a game, Kobe said: "I go home with my mother, my father, or

The Name Game

Kobe is an unusual first name. But it's not so unusual if you're a piece of beef. The young Laker star was named after a special cut of Japanese steak. Kobe steaks come from special cows that live in the area of Kobe Japan. His parents spotted the word on a menu at a steak house and liked the sound it made: *Ko - beee!* Mr. Bryant recalled that the restaurant was located in King of Prussia, Pennsylvania. "But I don't know if I should say that," Kobe's dad added, "because they might want the rights to his name!"

my sisters. We have a nice little dinner together. Then I go to sleep."

Kobe is no boring guy, though. He writes poetry and has recorded a hip-hop song. He also likes to have fun. He kids around with fans and even with the various reporters who

Musical Moves

Some observers have said that great basketball stars move with the grace of ballet dancers. Julius Erving and Michael Jordan were two of the best ever to leap above a basketball court. But how many big-time basketball stars have made a hip-hop record? Kobe has.

R&B singer Brian McKnight asked him to join in the remix of the song "Hold Me." The cut was recorded and released during the NBA's off-season in 1999. The pair also made a video together. But Kobe said there is no solo CD in his future — at least not yet.

"Right now, I'm too busy playing basketball to begin a serious recording career. Ball is my focus now," he told fans.

cover basketball. One day, a reporter remarked that he sometimes wore Kobe's signature shoes.

"Oh, yeah? How do you like them?" Kobe asked, smiling.

"Well, whatever plastic they use makes the shoes smell, and I have to keep them out in the garage," the reporter replied.

"You ever try changing your socks?" Kobe joked with a grin. The reporters laughed and high-fived after that one.

People expect a lot from Kobe on the basketball court. They will probably keep expecting a lot from him for a long time. That's okay. Kobe expects a great deal from himself too. When the game clock is running, he's deadly serious. He takes the ball, spins, whirls, soars, and slams! It's what "the next Jordan" is expected to do.

But Kobe is smart enough to enjoy himself as he lives his lifelong dream of NBA stardom. He takes basketball seriously, but he doesn't take himself too seriously. "I feel like a kid, and sometimes I feel like a grown-up," Kobe said. "I have the best of both worlds."

Dunkin' is what this guy does for a living, and how!

He's a cool one, this Tim Duncan. The San Antonio Spurs' young star is a very cool customer on the basketball court. Let other players wag their tongues, growl, or shriek. Tim simply plays the game. Let Allen Iverson create spine-tingling drama. Let Shaquille O'Neal demonstrate heavy-duty intensity with a backboard-shaking slam. Just give Tim a chance to do his thing with the ball and then *watch*.

He can do his thing, all right. In 1997-98, his rookie season, the 7' forward proved that he could do nearly everything on the court, offensively and defensively. He averaged 21.1 points, 11.9 rebounds, and 2.51 blocks per game to earn the NBA Rookie of the Year award. The next season, Tim won something even more important: the NBA playoff finals Most Valuable Player award.

Tim's most famous teammate, center David Robinson, was quite impressed after playing with Tim during only one season. "If Michael Jordan retires," David said in 1998, "then Tim is about the best player in the league."

TiM DUNCAN

Well, Michael Jordan — the King of the Court — *did* retire, in January 1999. In June, Tim helped the Spurs win the NBA title, which had *belonged* to Michael and his Chicago Bulls. Maybe it is time to crown a new, laidback ruler of the hoops. Maybe Tim Duncan will be the new King of the Court.

Hurricane Force

Tim comes from a tropical island in the Caribbean Sea, which is southeast of Florida. He was born on April 25, 1976, on the island of St. Croix *[croy]*. St. Croix is part of the United States Virgin Islands. It is a beautiful island, but very small. The population is about 55,000, which is roughly the size of a small U.S. city. Tim lived there with his mom, Ione, his dad, William, and his two sisters, Cheryl and Tricia.

As a kid, Tim never imagined becoming a great basketball star. No, he wanted to become a great Olympic swimmer! His older sister, Tricia, was an excellent swimmer. She competed in swimming at the 1988 Summer Olympic Games, in Seoul, South Korea. Tim wanted to be a great swimmer like Tricia. He might have made it, too. When he was only 13 years old, he was among the best of the U.S. kids in his age group at swimming the 400-meter freestyle. He seemed to be on track to make the Olympic team.

Then disaster struck — really. In 1989, a huge natural disaster changed Tim's life. Hurricane Hugo roared through St. Croix that year. The storm was so powerful it damaged about 80 percent of the buildings on the island. Hugo also wiped out the only Olympic-size pool there. Tim had no place to train.

That wasn't the worst of it. Tim's mother, Ione, had been ill when the hurricane hammered St. Croix. She was fighting a fierce battle against breast cancer. She needed regular chemotherapy treatments to survive. But when Hugo hit the island, the furious wind and water knocked out electricity all over St. Croix. With hospitals and roads damaged and power outages that lasted as long as two months, Mrs. Duncan couldn't receive her cancer treatments in a timely way. The cancer overwhelmed her and she died seven months after the storm hit.

Disaster and Devastation

As you can imagine, Tim was devastated by the death of his mother. Hurricane Hugo had destroyed large parts of his world. His Olympic dreams were also dead. What was left for him? What could he do?

First, Tim did what anyone would do. He grieved over the loss of his mother. Tim also felt disappointment over his swimming future. Eventually, though, Tim picked himself up and started to move on with his life. He found a new sport to throw his energies into: basketball.

Tim played organized basketball for the first time in the ninth grade. He played at St. Dunstan's Episcopal High School, in Christiansted, a port city in St. Croix. His talents developed quickly. Soon Tim was one of the most impressive, dominating players on the island.

Still, St. Croix is off the beaten track. College basketball coaches don't visit regularly looking for players with potential. But as it happened, in 1992, a group of young NBA

TiM DUNCAN

TiM'S TALE

BIRTH DATE: April 25, 1976
HEIGHT: 7' **WEIGHT:** 255 pounds
HOMES: San Antonio, Texas, and St. Croix, U.S.
Virgin Islands
**FAVORITE SPORT TO PLAY (OTHER THAN
BASKETBALL):** Football
FAVORITE ATHLETE: Former basketball great Magic
Johnson
FAVORITE FOOD: Steak
FAVORITE MUSIC: Reggae
FAVORITE BOOK: *Jurassic Park*, by Michael Crichton
BIGGEST FEARS: Sharks and high places

players visited St. Croix to promote their league. One rookie, Chris King, had played at Wake Forest University, in Winston-Salem, North Carolina. Chris saw Tim playing in St. Croix. He persuaded Wake Forest coach Dave Odom to check out this talented kid. Tim was just 16.

Soon, other schools heard about Tim, too. They wanted Tim to play for them. But Tim eventually settled on Wake Forest and started school there, in 1993.

At Wake Forest, Tim became one of the best college players in the country. He won the important Naismith and Wooden awards. He was named the 1996-97 NCAA National Player of the Year by the Associated Press, the U.S.

Basketball Writers, the *Sporting News*, the National Association of Basketball Coaches, and others! The Associated Press named him a First Team All-America.

And no wonder! Look at some of the things he did on the court: Tim blocked 481 shots to become the all-time leading shot-blocker in Atlantic Coast Conference history and second all-time in the entire NCAA. He was the first college player to: score more than 1,500 points, grab more than 1,000 rebounds, block more than 400 shots, *and* pass for more

Slammin' for Charity

Tim is a good guy, even off the court. He works actively with the Spurs Foundation, which benefits the United Way and the Children's Bereavement Center of San Antonio. The center assists children who lose a parent, as Tim did. He also donates 25 tickets to each home game so that kids who can't afford tickets may watch the Spurs live.

Tim also helps out NBA Team Up, an organization encourages young people to improve their community. And he is looking for ways to take sports and business opportunities to St. Croix.

than 200 assists in a career. He helped Wake Forest become the first team in 14 years to win back-to-back ACC championships. Pretty amazing stuff.

Nearly everyone thought that Tim would leave college after his junior year and join the NBA. He could easily have been the number 1 draft pick. But he didn't. When his mother was dying, she had made Tim and his sisters promise to earn college diplomas. Tim didn't want to break that promise. So he stayed at Wake Forest and graduated with a degree in psychology. His sisters also kept their promises to their mom.

Batman and Robin

After Tim graduated, the San Antonio Spurs chose him as the number 1 pick in the 1997 NBA draft. Getting Tim was a great move for the Spurs. They had finished sixth in their division in the 1996-97 season. They needed something more, and Tim was that something.

Tim had played center throughout high school and college. The Spurs already had a terrific center in David Robinson. Two centers on one team could have caused problems. But the coaches were smart enough to play Tim at forward, alongside David, who is 10 years older and much more experienced. That gave the team two tall, strong, talented men battling opponents side by side — the young rookie and the mighty veteran. They are sort of like Batman and Robin — only they're both tall!

Tim and David quickly became an effective combination against even the best teams. This double-trouble strategy worked because Tim and David found ways to work together. They became good friends, too. Right after the '97 NBA draft, David invited Tim to his home near Aspen, Colorado. Together they lifted weights and played one-on-one, with David offering advice and Tim listening.

"I've tried to help Tim understand that if you don't prepare yourself, you don't perform well," David said. Only halfway through his new buddy's rookie year, David announced that he would rather play with Tim than with any forward in the Western Conference, including veteran All-Star Karl Malone of the Utah Jazz!

Tim had a great first season. He was the only rookie selected for the 1998 All-Star Game. He won Rookie of the Month during each of the season's six months! And he received 113 of 116 votes in the NBA Rookie of the Year voting.

Mr. Modest

Tim's performance during the 1997-98 season justified all the awards, just as it had during his college career. He led the NBA with 57 double-doubles (games in which he gets 10 or more of two of the following: points, rebounds, blocks, assists, or steals). Tim scored in double figures 77 times, including fifty 20-point games and eight 30-point efforts. Tim was also among the NBA leaders in scoring, rebounding, shot-blocking, and field-goal percentage!

Through his success, Tim remained modest. When a fan asked about his transition to pro basketball, he said: "It's been a long season that has been tough at times. But I've had a lot of help, so it has been great. I'm learning but I have a long way to go." He also gave David plenty of credit for offering advice and lessons during that rookie year.

People sometimes criticized Tim because of his laidback manner. But Tim's cool style obviously works just fine on a basketball court. It doesn't mean that Tim lacks feelings, or isn't trying, or that he doesn't laugh and have fun. Far from it. He sometimes wears his practice shorts backward, for instance. And he has two tattoos: a magician and a wizard. Tim keeps others loose when they're on the road.

"He busts into my room on road trips and, if there's a basketball game on, he makes me turn to wrestling," recalled Antonio Daniels, a Spur guard and Tim's best friend. "We're in each other's rooms hours a day, watching TV and laughing."

One other little-known fact about Tim: He is the Spurs' video-game champion! Forward Sean Elliott had been the team's undisputed video king — until he invited a rookie named Tim Duncan to his house.

"You have to understand, I don't lose at home. I'm King Video. When the neighborhood kids come around to play, I make it a point to destroy them," Sean said. "None of the other guys on the team can come close to me. But then this rookie comes along and he humbles me. He made me go out and buy a game manual so I can study the moves more." In Tim's own home, he has so much video-game equipment, it doesn't all fit into one room!

But life isn't all video games for Tim. He works hard at basketball. Even after his astounding rookie season, he worked hard. He understood that work was the only way to keep the sharp edge on his talent. His pal David Robinson knew this, too. Following the strike that shortened the 1998-99 season by 32 games, Tim and David were two of only three players with contracts who showed up for the Spurs' first voluntary workout. This was after almost eight months away from the game.

Once official competition finally got underway, Tim's pre-season efforts really paid off. With David at his side, he helped make 1999 a memorable year for San Antonio fans, at last. The Spurs had a reputation as a team with talent, just not quite enough talent to make it all the way. For 10 years, they had struggled to get into the NBA Finals. Each year they somehow fell short. This was a huge frustration for all the Spurs, especially David.

But with Tim in his second season with the team, things finally changed. He put up high individual numbers, just as he had during his rookie year. He was the only NBA player who ranked among the Top 10 in each of these categories: scoring (sixth), rebounding (fifth), blocked shots (seventh), and field-goal percentage (eighth)!

What's more, he showed himself to be capable of coming up with a really Big Game. For example, in April 1999, he scored a career-high 39 points in a 103–91 win over the Vancouver Grizzlies. Tim sank 13 of those points in the third quarter alone! He also had 13 rebounds and six blocked shots in the game. That kind of huge performance can be key during the playoffs.

The Spurs rolled through the regular season and into the NBA Finals for the first time. There they faced the New York Knicks. The Knicks had a problem: Their best player, All-Star center Patrick Ewing, was out with a serious injury. But they had two even bigger problems: Tim and David were healthy!

With San Antonio leading the Finals series three games to one, the fifth game grew tense. New York was battling to keep its season alive. Tim and David had used their size and skill all game long to control the basket, offensively and

Name That Star

By late 1999, fans and players were still looking for the right nickname for Tim. David Robinson, who attended the U.S. Naval Academy, is called "the Admiral." Should Tim be "the General" or what? One teammate, Mario Elie, called Tim either the "Big Easy" or the "Quiet Assassin." "Merlin" is another nickname.

Even Tim's official website at www.slam-duncan.com was looking for just the right nickname. The website asked fans to choose among "the Big Easy," "the Cruzan Illusion," "Cash Flow," and "Magnum V.I."

But we think they might have missed the best name of all, even if it is a bit obvious. How about "Slam Duncan"?

defensively. But with little time left to play, the Spurs were ahead by only 1 point. The Knicks could still win and avoid elimination.

There were just 2.1 seconds left on the clock. The Knicks had the ball and threw it inbounds to Latrell Sprewell, who was standing under the basket. Latrell tried hard to break free for a good shot. Against most teams, he would have succeeded, too. But not against the Spurs, with Tim and David ganging up on him. An instant later, the final buzzer sounded. The Knicks' last-ditch effort to score had failed. San Antonio had won, 78–77. They were the NBA champions!

A New King

Tim was brilliant that NBA Finals series. He had 27.4 points, 14 rebounds, and 2.1 blocked shots per game to earn the Finals MVP trophy. Shortly after the decisive game, David wrote a story for *Sports Illustrated*. "It's also a great feeling to have Tim Duncan by my side," David wrote. "He's obviously the best player in the league. Tim was phenomenal against New York, and his Finals MVP award was well-deserved."

A year earlier, David had said Tim *might* become "the best player in the league." Now he was convinced. Tim had risen to the top with his overwhelming display during the Finals. No one needed Michael Jordan to make the championship series special this time around.

The basketball court seemed to have its new unofficial ruler. King Michael was gone. Long live King Tim!

SUPER 8 MiA HAMM

It isn't just love of the game that makes Mia great

Mia Hamm is all about hard work, dedication to winning, and love — love of soccer and love of her family. Mia's deep feelings for the game grew out of her even deeper feelings for her family. And, in turn, Mia's family memories help inspire her great play.

Those two parts of Mia's life came together in a single game after the death of her beloved older brother, Garrett. In 1997, Garrett died after years of fighting a rare blood disorder. He was just 28 years old. Garrett had been the reason Mia was drawn to soccer as a kid. He had helped give his sister the confidence she needed to compete successfully as a young athlete. But now Garrett was gone.

At the time Garrett died, Mia was playing in the U.S. Women's Soccer Team's victory tour. She missed two games after Garrett died. Then Mia decided the best way to honor her brother was to pull herself together as much as possible and play soccer. It was what he would have wanted her to do. So Mia rejoined the team, in Tampa, Florida. She arrived just in time for matches against the team from South Korea.

The first game was played in heavy rain. Despite the weather, there was a sellout crowd that included Garrett's widow, Cherylynn.

Mia was playing the game for Garrett. She wanted to play her best. Unknown to Mia, her teammates had decided to attach black armbands to their uniforms in memory of Garrett. When Mia saw this thoughtful gesture by her friends, she was deeply moved. By the time the game started, Mia was feeling so many emotions. One had to wonder how she could play at all. But she did — and how!

Inspired by Garrett

Mia is a forward, known for her quick moves and lightning speed down the field. Playing for Garrett inspired her and she quickly seized control of the game. Only 49 seconds into the match, Mia scored her first goal!

Seventeen minutes later, she scored again. When all was said and done, Mia was on the field for 54 of the game's 60 minutes, despite the torrential rain. Her two early goals had sparked the team to a 7–0 victory. Mia had given her best, just as she had hoped to do.

Later, she explained that something had felt different during the game. Mia said she knew that someone she loved and missed terribly was watching over her. It was a feeling that she would have every time she stepped onto a soccer field after that. "Now, no matter where I play, I feel Garrett is there," she said.

Mia is the best soccer player in the world, although she is

A MIA MOMENT

BIRTH DATE: March 17, 1972

HEIGHT: 5' 5"   **WEIGHT:** 125 pounds

HOME: Chapel Hill, North Carolina

FAVORITE SPORTS TO PLAY (OTHER THAN SOCCER):
Golf, basketball

FAVORITE SPORT TO WATCH (OTHER THAN SOCCER):
College basketball

FAVORITE ATHLETES: Hockey player Wayne Gretzky, cyclist Greg LeMond, and heptathlete and long jumper Jackie Joyner-Kersee

FAVORITE FOOD: Italian

FAVORITE ALBUM: "The Joshua Tree" by U2

PLACE SHE WOULD MOST LIKE TO VISIT: Australia

SUPERSTITION: Always ties her right shoelace first before games

SECRET DESIRE: To play on the women's pro golf tour

too modest to agree with such high praise. More important — at least to her — Mia has helped make her team, the U.S. Women's Soccer Team, the best in the world. Mia has helped the team win the biggest titles in the sport: the Olympic gold medal in 1996 and the World Cup in 1991 and 1999.

All this has made Mia famous, but she doesn't like attention. She hates talking to the news media. She can't avoid it, though, especially after all the hoopla over the big 1999

World Cup win. Mia is a star, whether she likes it or not. And so she has turned the burden of being famous into an opportunity to be a role model for kids and an ambassador for women's soccer. She reaches out to young girls, in particular.

"We want to get girls out to the games to see how hard we play and how fast we play. We want them to see the chemistry and intensity," Mia said. "It's another choice for them. They can say, 'I want to be a nurse.' 'I want to be a doctor.' 'I want to be a professional soccer player.' "

Being the kind of professional soccer player that Mia is would be a worthy goal for any young person, male or female. Mia always puts her team first while giving everything she's got as an individual player. She never grandstands or grabs the glory. She just plays lots of great soccer, and then shares the credit with her teammates. Mia is an excellent example to anyone who wants to be a great athlete, or a great person.

Borrowed from a Ballerina

Mia was born in Selma, Alabama, on March 17, 1972, St. Patrick's Day! She is the fourth of Stephanie and Bill Hamm's six children. Her real name is Mariel Margaret Hamm, but early on she became known as Mia. The nickname was borrowed from a ballerina who had taught her mother. Mrs. Hamm loved ballet. When Mia was 5 years old, Mrs. Hamm wanted her to take ballet lessons. But Mia resisted. She wanted to play soccer, instead!

Mia's siblings included Garrett, who was about three years older than she. Garrett was an orphan who was part

American and part Thai (the people from Thailand, a country in southeast Asia). He had been adopted by the Hamms when he was 8. Mia adored Garrett and copied everything he did. One of Garrett's favorite activities was soccer. He was good at it too. This helped attract Mia to the game.

The neighborhood kids played soccer and other sports. Mia tried to join in. "When they would play pickup football and start choosing teams, nobody wanted Mia because she was too little," Mrs. Hamm recalled. "But Garrett knew she had a great ability to catch the ball and hold it and run with it." Her brother's belief in Mia's athletic abilities helped give her the courage to play with other kids.

When she was 5 years old, Mia joined a peewee soccer team. Her talent soon was obvious: She began to score goals. For the next 10 years, she played soccer with the boys. She was usually the only girl. But she loved the sport too much to mind. And she was so good that the boys — at least those on her team — didn't mind.

Mia was a shy child, except at home. With so many kids in the family, Mia couldn't be too quiet there. Sometimes she felt shouting was the only way to be heard. "I was never very good at expressing myself. I was this really emotional kid — still am — and I would get attention by screaming and yelling," she recalled. "When I would get frustrated or upset, I didn't know how to step out of it and say 'Okay, Mia, let's think about what you say before you say it.' I was always the one apologizing later."

But Mia had nothing to apologize for on the soccer field. When Mia was 14 and living in Texas, a local coach asked his friend Anson Dorrance to come and check out this amazing young soccer player. Mr. Dorrance coached the University of North Carolina women's soccer team and the U.S. national team. He had seen good soccer players. But the first time he saw Mia was something else.

So, *That's* How It Feels!

Mia usually plays forward — up front, where she can torment the other team's goalie. But once, Mia played way back at the other end of the field and got a taste of what it's like facing scorers like herself. She filled in as goalie for the U.S. national team!

During a 1991 World Cup match against Denmark, goalkeeper Briana Scurry was ejected for a foul. The U.S. had already used all its substitutions, so it could not put in another goalie. Mia was picked to step in for Briana for a few minutes! "I was scared to death," Mia remembered. "I hope I don't have to do it again." Despite her fears, Mia made one save, and the United States ended up winning the game.

"I saw this young kid accelerate like she was shot out of a cannon," Coach Dorrance said. "Without seeing her touch the ball, I ran around saying 'Is that Mia Hamm?' "

It was Mia Hamm, all right. At 15, she joined the national team — its youngest member ever! Coaches were impressed with her raw talent and speed. Still, Mia's move to top-flight competition was hard. "Tactically, I didn't know what to do," Mia said. "During fitness sessions, I was dying [because they were so hard]. I would cry half the time."

But Mia stuck it out. She learned and improved, but it took some time. She didn't score a goal until her 17th international match, in 1990!

After high school graduation, Mia followed Coach Dorrance to the University of North Carolina (UNC), in the town of Chapel Hill. She soon became one of the best college players in the country. UNC won the national championship each season Mia played for the team — four straight years! She set the national record for goals scored in a career, with 103. She won the award as the best female college soccer player in the country twice.

During her college years, Mia also played on the national team that won the very first women's World Cup, in 1991. The U.S. beat China, 2–1, on goals by Michelle Akers.

Mia graduated in 1994 with her political-science degree. But politics wasn't on her mind. Two other subjects were — marriage and soccer. She was married in 1994 to college classmate Christian Corey. Christian became a Marine Corps helicopter pilot. Mia trained hard to improve her soccer game.

Women's soccer had never been a medal sport in the

Olympics. When it was announced that it would be a medal sport at the 1996 Summer Games, in Atlanta, Georgia, Mia and her teammates were stoked! They set their sights on one goal — an Olympic gold medal. The members of the team spent a lot of time together, training hard. They also trained hard on their own. "It is an awesome group of women committed to winning, growing soccer in America, and setting a good example for young athletes everywhere," Mia said.

The intense efforts by Mia and her teammates paid off. After playing five games, the U.S. faced China in the final. The stadium was filled with 76,481 screaming, cheering fans. The pressure was on. No problem. Mia and her fellow Americans delivered, against the tough Chinese team. Just as they had in the World Cup in 1991, the U.S. women's soccer team defeated the team from China, 2–1. The U.S. women had their gold medals!

Mia was a hot property. Requests for interviews flooded in. Product-endorsement offers piled up. But Mia still didn't enjoy the attention. Gradually, she got used to it as she gave more interviews and appeared on television. She also was featured in advertisements. She wrote a fitness column for *USA Weekend* magazine. She even had her own signature sneaker, the Nike Air Zoom M9. (Mia wears number 9 on her jersey.) Mia got Nike to stamp her brother Garrett's initials, GJH, on the sole of each pair.

Mia had won individual and team awards. She was the first player — male or female — ever named U.S. Soccer Athlete of the Year three times. (She won the award from

1994-96.) On May 22nd, 1999, when she scored her 108th goal, Mia became the highest scoring player in international soccer history.

But the 1999 World Cup was coming up. It would be a big tournament for the U.S. Team, in some ways bigger than any World Cup before. That's because the finals would take place in the United States. The noisy home crowd would be rooting for a second world championship. The U.S. had lost

Lookin' Good

People magazine once named Mia one of the 50 most beautiful people in the world. Mia disagreed. "It's obvious that I'm not," she said. Many people think the magazine got it right, though. Said her teammate, Julie Foudy: "Mia has natural beauty. It's not something she has to spend a thousand dollars on."

Advertisers think Mia has something special that can help sell their products. Her face has turned up in many ads, for everything from Gatorade to Barbie dolls.

One thing is for sure: She looks great dashing downfield with a soccer ball on her foot and the opponent's goal in her eyes!

in the semi-finals of the previous World Cup, in 1995, to Norway. The U.S. women really wanted the Cup back

Mia's performance during the 1999 World Cup wasn't up to her usual standards. She scored twice in the first two games, then had a long streak without a goal through the team's next three games. Mia began to doubt herself, to wonder why she wasn't scoring. But she concentrated on being the great team player she had always been, and she remained the key to the U.S. attack.

The final game of the 1999 Women's World Cup was amazing! It was played in the Rose Bowl, in California. More than 90,000 people crowded into the famous old stadium, setting a new world attendance record for a women's sports event. Forty million more tuned in to watch.

Just as they had at the 1996 Olympics, China and the U.S. faced off for the championship. The two teams fought back and forth, but no one scored during regular play. No one scored during overtime either! That meant there would be a penalty-kick shoot-out to decide the gold medal!

In a shoot-out, five players from each team take turns going one-on-one against the goalie. The goalie must stand on the goal line without moving her feet until the ball is kicked. After every player had a turn, the team with the highest number of goals wins.

The situation was tense as one player after another stepped up to the ball. The score was tied at two goals each when China's midfielder, Liu Ying, faced off against U.S. goalkeeper Briana Scurry. Ying hammered the ball, but Briana dove to her left to make an amazing save! The crowd went wild. The save gave the U.S. women the chance they needed. Unless they missed a shot, they would win.

Each team scored again, to make it 3–3. Mia was up next. The pressure was terrible. Mia, who had been struggling, didn't want to blow her team's chance for a gold medal. So she suggested that another player take her place in the shoot-out, but it was too late! She had to take the kick.

Mia walked on to the field, knowing she had to find her missing confidence. If she made her shot, it would put the U.S. ahead going into the final round of penalty kicks. Mia concentrated, stepped swiftly into the ball, and blasted her shot. It was perfect: Another goal for the United States! Mia had come through when it really counted.

China scored again after Mia's kick. With the scored tied 4–4, Brandi Chastain of the U.S. nailed one past goalie Goa Hong of China. The U.S. had won the shoot-out, 5–4, and won the World Cup title!

Courage Under Fire

It takes courage to do what Mia did that day — to stand before the world and give your best, even when you aren't playing your best. That kind of courage, strong character, and team spirit are part of the reason Mia remains the all-time greatest female soccer player.

Inspired by her brother Garrett, Mia continues to shred defenses and terrify goalies around the world. She may be shy about publicity and modest about her talent. But she is something else too, something all true athletes want to become: Mia Hamm is the very best in her sport.

SUPER 8 KEN GRIFFEY, JUNIOR

Dazzling fielding and slugging make the Kid a hit

They call him Junior or, sometimes, just the Kid. Either nickname fits this grown-up baseball player, even now, as he gets ready to bat in one of the most famous arenas in the world.

Ken Griffey, Junior, digs into the batter's box at Yankee Stadium, in New York City. He grinds his high-top cleats into the dirt and stares at the pitcher without blinking. It's May 8, 1999, and, as usual, sportswriters and photographers in the stadium are watching carefully. The fans and players pay attention too. They know that at any time, Junior may do something special. This is a player on his way to the Baseball Hall of Fame. No one wants to miss a feat that may take him a step closer.

Junior doesn't appear worried about the attention. The Seattle Mariner slugger rarely looks worried when he's on a baseball field. Smiles, laughter, and fun are more his style. Why, just before he walked to home plate, he was kneeling in the on-deck circle, just looking around the stands. He wasn't studying the pitcher. He was checking out the fans

KEN GRIFFEY, JR.

GRIFFEY AT A GLANCE

BIRTH DATE: November 21, 1969

HEIGHT: 6' 3"   **WEIGHT:** 205 pounds

BATS: Left   **THROWS:** Left

FAMILY: Melissa (wife); Trey (son), born January 19, 1994; Taryn (daughter), born October 21, 1995

HOME: Issaquah, Washington

FAVORITE SPORT TO PLAY (OTHER THAN BASEBALL): Golf

FAVORITE SPORT TO WATCH (OTHER THAN BASEBALL): Basketball

FAVORITE CLOTHES: Jeans and sweat suits

FAVORITE ANIMAL: Dogs (owns three Rottweilers)

behind the Mariners' dugout. Junior could have been a Little Leaguer preparing for routine batting practice rather than a major league star!

Now, Junior stands at the plate and waits quietly for the pitch, his face relaxed. His powerful hands and arms wave the bat around in tight circles, poised for action. New York Yankee pitcher Jay Tessmer stares in at catcher Jorge Posada for the sign.

Jay slices his first pitch across the inside corner of the plate. Junior watches it sail by. Strike one! Jay has faced Junior twice before in his career — and both times he got this slugger out. Can he do it again?

Junior doesn't let the second pitch go by. This time, he takes his trademark short stride into the ball and connects with a loud *thwack!* Junior's hands explode through the swing, propelling his black bat around and upward. The baseball soars in a beautiful arc and lands in the rightfield seats. *Home run!* It is his 361st career homer, and it ties him for 45th place on the all-time home-run list. Who is he tied with? None other than the legendary Yankee great Joe DiMaggio! Way to go, Junior!

The Best in the Game

After the game, the reporters want to know what Junior thinks about catching up with Joe DiMaggio. Junior says that he didn't know the home run meant anything special until after he hit it. "I was sitting in the dugout when a cameraman leaned in and told me," he says, and then adds: "It's nice, but it was more important we won the game, more than any homer, even one that tied me with a great player like DiMaggio."

These feelings tell you a lot about Junior. He's a ballplayer who loves the game and loves to win. He thinks about his team first. He works very hard, but enjoys himself every day at the park. He is modest about his achievements, and they are many. Junior has shown such huge talent that many people, people who understand baseball, believe he is the best in the game.

"When you look at what Junior has done and the skills he possesses, you have to say that in this era, he is as good as anyone who has played," says Lou Piniella, manager of the

KEN GRIFFEY, JR.

Seattle Mariners. "I can't think of any player in the past thirty years to compare with Junior."

A Chip Off the Old Block

You could go back almost three decades to see where Junior's baseball skills started. His father, Ken Griffey, Senior, was a fine major league ballplayer in the 1970's and '80s *(see box on page 67)*. That meant that Junior — who was born in 1969 — grew up around the best baseball in the world. He had a great coach nearby: his dad!

"He had shortcuts — like my teaching him how to hit, how to turn on the ball, how to stay out of slumps," Ken senior once told *Sports Illustrated*. "When [Junior] started coming of age and doing things he shouldn't . . . he'd get sent to me. I'd give him a good talking-to, then take him under the stands at Yankee Stadium, and throw him batting practice. That's where he really learned to play the game."

Ken senior grew up in Donora, Pennsylvania, as one of six children in a poor family. His father left the family when Ken was just 2 years old. Ken was athletic. He worked hard at baseball, and at supporting his family, even as a kid.

Although he played several sports well, Ken decided to concentrate on baseball. He turned pro after high school and spent almost five years in the minor leagues before getting a chance to play with the Cincinnati Reds in 1973. He became a key member of the Reds teams that won the World Series in 1975 and 1976.

As an important player on a successful ball club, Ken earned good money. As a result, Ken junior had no money problems, a very different experience than his dad had known. Junior sometimes rode in a Rolls Royce to Little League games. His first car was a $30,000 BMW!

Junior's mother was also athletic. Alberta "Birdie" Griffey played basketball and volleyball. She had six brothers and sisters. Her father worked at a steel mill. Birdie married Ken senior right out of high school, before he was even playing pro baseball. They lived through some tough years with little money before Ken hit the big time.

George Kenneth Griffey, Junior, their first child, was born in Donora on November 21, 1969. Ken senior had just finished his rookie season in the minors. He was only 19 years old — the very age Junior would be when *he* broke into the major leagues! Later, Junior was joined by a brother, Craig, and then a sister, Lathesia.

By the time Junior was 3, he was playing Wiffle ball, and later he starred in the Reds' annual father-son baseball games. When he started playing organized baseball, Junior dominated. In Little League, he threw so hard that opposing hitters sometimes cried because they were afraid of being hit by his pitches. When he was 16, Junior competed against 18-year-olds in Connie Mack League Baseball. He smashed three homers in the league's 1986 World Series!

Junior didn't start playing for his school team until his junior year in high school. He became a star anyway. He set several records and attracted many major league scouts at Archbishop Moeller High, in Cincinnati, Ohio. On June 2, 1987, the Seattle Mariners made Junior the first person chosen in that year's major league draft of amateur players.

KEN GRIFFEY, JR.

THE SENIOR GRIFFEY

Ken senior was not a superstar, as his son has become. But he was one of the fastest runners and most dependable hitters on one of the greatest teams in baseball history! From 1973 through 1981, Ken hit .311 and stole 150 bases for the Cincinnati Reds. In 1976, when he hit .336, he almost won the National League batting title. Together with talented teammates such as Pete Rose, Johnny Bench, Joe Morgan, and others, he led the "Big Red Machine" to World Series wins in 1975 and 1976.

Ken later played for the New York Yankees, the Atlanta Braves, and the Reds again (from 1988 to 1990). Then, on August 29, 1990, he was signed by the Mariners. Senior and Junior became the first father-son combo to play for the same major league team at the same time. Ken senior retired after the 1991 season. He finished with a .296 career batting average and 200 stolen bases, and 2,143 hits over 19 seasons.

They gave him a $160,000 bonus when he signed a contract with them. Junior was only 17.

Junior started out at the lowest level of minor league ball, Rookie League. He had never lived away from home. He was in for a big shock during his first year in the minors.

Junior played in Bellingham, Washington, about 90 miles north of Seattle. His team rode to the games on a 30-year-old bus. Some trips took 10 hours! But it wasn't just the length of the trip. Junior told reporters that one of the bus driver's sons called him racist names and another son threatened to gun him down. "I didn't know what to do," Junior recalled. "All I knew is I wanted to go home."

The problems affected Junior's play. He performed poorly, and he didn't hustle on the field. It looked as if he didn't want to be there. But his mother came to see him to find out what was wrong. She sternly urged him to tough it out and concentrate on his career. He did, and ended the season with strong numbers: a .313 batting average, 14 homers, and 43 runs batted in. *Baseball America* magazine named Junior the top prospect in the minors.

Junior was still struggling with his feelings, though. When he returned home after his rookie year, he began to have arguments with his father. Ken senior expected Junior to be responsible and move to his own apartment or pay rent to his parents. "I was confused," Junior later told *The Seattle Times*. "I was hurting, and I wanted to cause some hurt for others."

Junior was so unhappy and confused that he did a terrible thing. In January 1988, he tried to commit suicide by swallowing 277 aspirin pills! He threw up. His girlfriend's mother raced him to the hospital and afterward, he was fine.

Junior doesn't discuss his attempt to kill himself any more. After all, it happened a long time ago when he was still a teenager. But he did speak to a reporter about it once

Junior "Bats" .500!

There are nearly 30 Internet sites dedicated to Junior, but he sponsors his own site, on America Online. He puts "Junior's Journal" on the site so fans can read his thoughts about baseball and anything else on his mind.

In the June 8, 1999, journal entry, Junior stuck his neck out with two bold sports predictions. He said that Tiger Woods would win the U.S. Open golf tournament and that the San Antonio Spurs would nab the NBA championship. Junior was right about the Spurs. They defeated the New York Knicks in the NBA Finals. But Tiger did not win the U.S. Open. (Payne Stewart did.) Half right isn't so bad, though. As a fortune teller, you could say that Junior is batting .500!

because he wanted others to learn from him that suicide is *never* the right solution to troubles in your life.

Father and son began to have long talks after this. They settled many of the problems between them. As Junior settled down emotionally, his game improved. In the 1988 season, Junior moved on with his career in a big way. He performed well and swiftly rose through the minor leagues, playing for teams in California and Vermont.

Junior was invited to the Mariner training camp, before the 1989 season. There, he continued to come on strong. He set a Mariner spring training record by getting at least one hit in 15 straight games. He also swatted his way to team records for hits and RBIs, batting an impressive .359 in the exhibition season. And he played brilliantly on defense.

Still, the coaches weren't sure this kid was ready for the pressure of daily big-league play. He had only been through two years in the minors, after all. And he was just 19. But Junior felt sure. He knew there was still much to learn, but he also felt confident about tackling the major leagues. Finally, Manager Jim Lefebvre *[le-FEE-ver]* announced his decision to this budding baseball star: "Congratulations! You're my starting centerfielder," he told Junior in March.

Junior was delighted. And so was his dad, because this news fulfilled a dream for both Ken Griffeys. They would become the first father and son to play in the major leagues at the same time!

April 3, 1989, was the historic day. Ken senior played for the Cincinnati Reds, against the Los Angeles Dodgers. Junior played for the Mariners, against the Oakland A's. Dad did

KEN GRIFFEY, JR.

not get a hit that day. Junior did. In his first official major league at-bat, he smacked a double off Oakland ace Dave Stewart. It was just the beginning.

A Record Breaker

During his first 11 seasons in the majors, Junior set more records and earned more important honors than anyone expected. Even Junior himself couldn't have anticipated so much success so fast. Let the numbers from his first 11 seasons (through 1999) tell the story:

• In 1997 and 1998, Junior hammered 56 home runs. No, not 56 total; 56 in each season! That was after hitting 49 in 1996. In 1999, he hit 48.

• He smashed 14 grand slams.

• He hit 398 career homers and, at age 29, was just shy of reaching the 400-homer milestone.

And he has done all this despite missing 51 games in the 1994 season due to the baseball strike and another 73 games the following year after breaking two bones in his left wrist.

The statistics go on and on:

• Junior batted over .300 six times between 1989 and 1999.

• In 1998, he became just the third player to have more than 140 RBIs three seasons in a row. The other ballplayers who accomplished this feat were Babe Ruth and Lou Gehrig — pretty good company!

• Junior also stole 20 bases for the first time in 1998, and then stole 24 in 1999.

Junior is an outstanding defensive player as well. Through

1998, he had won nine Gold Glove awards in a row for fielding excellence.

But Junior had done amazing things before. In 1997, he helped the Mariners win a team-record 90 games. He led the A.L. with 56 home runs and 147 RBIs. So that year, sportswriters named him the A.L.'s Most Valuable Player.

Fans love Junior. Starting in 1990, Junior was voted onto nine consecutive All-Star teams. Four of those times he was elected by wider margins than anyone in the majors. Fans find Junior exciting to watch, at bat and in the field. They feel that he makes the game fun.

Still Having Fun

All these things are true, and one big reason might be that Junior has held on to the kid in himself. The multimillionaire slugger still calls his father *collect* to make him pay the bill. He plays video games and listens to rap music. He still brings his joy in playing baseball to the ballpark. During warm-ups, he often wears his cap backward. He kids his teammates. Most days, Junior wears a broad grin as he strides across the field.

"When I was growing up, my dad always told me, 'Have fun,' " Junior said. " 'Don't worry if you make an out. Just do the best job you can.' "

And that is what Junior does, month after month, year after year — even when times are tough for him or for his team. His "best job" has been outstanding. The ability to be outstanding day in and day out have made Junior a true star.

SUPER 8 MARK McGWIRE

A record-breaking slugger makes his Mark as a good dad

The baseball world had waited 37 years for this moment. And the wait was worth it. No fan who watched what happened in St. Louis, Missouri, on September 8, 1998, will ever forget it.

The big, red-headed man strode to the plate, his bat squeezed in his massive hands. Every camera in Busch Stadium was focused on him. That was nothing new. For weeks, each swing of Mark McGwire's bat had been accompanied by the whir of TV cameras and the explosion of 10,000 photo flashes. But, as it turned out, this moment *was* something new — for baseball, for the country, and for Mark.

It was the fourth inning of a game between Mark's St. Louis Cardinals and the Chicago Cubs. There were two outs, no one on base. The time was exactly 8:18 p.m. Millions of people across the country had tuned in to the TV broadcast to see what would happen. The most famous record in American sports was on the line. The pressure was on Mark big time.

73

Mark stepped into the batter's box, stared at Cub pitcher Steve Trachsel, and waited. Mark intercepted the first pitch, uncorking a mighty swing that smacked the ball in a low line-drive toward the leftfield corner. Mark sprinted for first base, one eye on the ball. He saw it clear the wall, just inside the foul pole. *Home run!* Mark had broken Roger Maris's home-run record! Big Mac had become the first major league player in history to hit 62 homers in a single season.

The stadium erupted in wild cheers as Mark leaped over first base in his excitement, missing the bag. Laughing, he went back and tagged first base, then bounded around the rest of the base paths. All of his Cardinal teammates were standing at home plate, waiting to congratulate him. His 10-year-old son, Matt, was there too, holding his dad's bat. Grinning, Mark picked his son up, lifting Matt high into the air.

Then Big Mac did something that no one expected. He ran into the front row of seats and hugged several of Roger Maris's children! (Roger had died in 1985, but all six of his children were in St. Louis to witness the historic homer.)

Mark also embraced Cub slugger Sammy Sosa *(see page 85)*. Sammy had hit almost as many home runs as Mark that season and would hit *his* 62nd homer, on September 13. Together, Sammy and Mark had staged a great race to see which one of them would break Roger's record. It was the greatest home-run chase in baseball history.

Mark won the race and ended the season with an amazing 70 homers. (Sammy finished with 66.) Mark and Sammy also earned the respect of a nation — not just for blasting home runs. It became clear that Mark was also a

MAC FACTS

BIRTH DATE: November 21, 1969
HEIGHT: 6' 5"   **WEIGHT:** 250 pounds
BATS: Right   **THROWS:** Right
HOMES: St. Louis, Missouri and Long Beach, California
FAVORITE HAT: Fishing hat
FAVORITE PERSON: His son, Matt
FREQUENT FOOD: Eats more than three pounds of red meat weekly.
EYESIGHT: Very bad! Without contacts, it's 20/500, which means that when he looks at something 20 feet away, he sees what most people see from 500 feet!
TEETH: Very good! He has never had any cavities.

special person. He talked publicly about overcoming serious problems in his life. He openly displayed his deep love for his son. He gave millions of dollars to help abused and neglected children. And he handled the intense daily pressure of the home run race with strength and modesty.

"Mark is a better person than he is a player," said Cardinal manager Tony LaRussa. That's quite a compliment, considering what a good player Mark is!

Mark kept things exciting in 1999. He homered six times in the final seven games to end up with 65. Before 1998, that number had seemed out of reach!

Mark's accomplishments reminded everyone how much

fun baseball can be. With Sammy, he helped to make the sport fun again. Starting in August 1994, a labor strike in baseball canceled the playoffs and the World Series. Many fans were turned off by the labor problems and stopped being baseball fans, even after the strike ended in April 1995. But the fun and excitement of 1998's Great Home Run Chase turned a lot of people back into baseball fans.

Mark, too, had had some rough times before he reached this high point in his career. There had been times along the way when he almost quit professional baseball. Mark McGwire's story is the tale of a long, successful battle against injuries and self-doubt.

The McGwire Men

Mark David McGwire was born in Pomona, California, on October 1, 1963. That happened to be exactly two years after Roger Maris slammed his 61st home run! Roger's smash broke Babe Ruth's 34-year-old record of 60 homers in one season.

Mark was the third of five boys, all big kids with huge appetites. Mark and his brothers all grew up to become at least 6' 3" and 220 pounds. They also became fine athletes: Dan was a pro football quarterback; Mike competed in high school golf and soccer; Bob was a standout golfer for his college team. The youngest brother, Jay, starred in several sports before a BB-gun accident blinded him in one eye when he was a teenager. He then became a personal trainer. Mark grew to be 6' 5" and 250 pounds, one of the biggest players in major league baseball.

MARK MCGWIRE

The McGwire boys' father, John, was a big, athletic man too. He was 6' 3" and 225 pounds in 1998 at the age of 61. As a child, Mr. McGwire had suffered from polio, a crippling disease that left him with one leg much shorter than the other. But he still boxed in college and learned to play excellent golf. He later became a dentist and settled down in Southern California with his wife, Ginger.

Though he loved sports, Mr. McGwire didn't want Mark to learn bad habits or take baseball too seriously when he was very young. So he decided not to let 7-year-old Mark play Little League baseball. But Mark cried so hard when he heard that he couldn't play that Mr. McGwire gave in the next year. Mark's very first Little League at-bat was a sign of things to come: He belted a home run!

Mark was a shy boy who just happened to play baseball well. He was "the kind of kid who liked to sit in the back of the room and just blend in," he told *Sports Illustrated*. "I was always just a basic athlete, nothing extraordinary. But I was a hard worker. And I liked to do a lot of that work where people couldn't see me. I'd throw balls against a cement wall or set a ball on a tee and hit it."

Mark was modest about his accomplishments. He hid his trophies inside a closet because they embarrassed him. He was also generous — perhaps too generous. Often Mark would give away his belongings to friends: baseball gloves, shirts, a sweater. Once he even donated his shoes to a buddy. "I gave 'em to Stan," he explained to his mother. "He needed 'em."

In high school, Mark was an outstanding pitcher. He

HOMER MANIA

Big Mac and Slammin' Sammy Sosa weren't the only players knocking truckloads of baseballs out of the stadium in the late 1990's. Ken Griffey, Junior; Jose Canseco; Greg Vaughn; and Juan Gonzalez were among a pack of other big boppers.

So many players hit homers that some people wondered if the balls were "juiced," or altered in some way, to produce more home runs. But most players and experts believed there were some other reasons for all the home runs:

- There were more smaller stadiums;
- More players were bigger and stronger;
- The umpires were calling a smaller strike zone, so batters were getting better pitches to hit;
- Because there were more baseball teams, the pitching talent was stretched thin. That meant batters were getting more pitches that were easy to hit.

continued to pitch in college. At the University of Southern California (USC), he pitched on the same team with a tall kid named Randy Johnson. Randy, of course, went on to fame as a pitcher with the Seattle Mariners and the Arizona Diamondbacks.

But Ron Vaughn, one of Mark's coaches at USC, saw something else in the young ballplayer. He thought Mark had the potential to be a great hitter. Coach Vaughn worked with Mark on his batting stance and swing. During his junior year, Mark hit 32 homers in 67 games! That settled it: Mark's days on the mound were over. He gave up pitching so that he could focus full-time on batting.

And Mark's days in college were over, too. After his junior year, Mark was selected by the Oakland A's in the first round of the 1984 baseball draft. Then things got a little rough for him. He was sent to play in the lowest levels of the minor leagues, but he struggled to hit anything, much less a home run. He struck out often and fielded poorly. Mark was so stunned and upset by these failures that he thought seriously about giving up. Kathy Williamson, who was married to Mark at the time, recalled those dark times. "I can remember lying in bed in the middle of the night and hearing Mark say, 'I can't hit the baseball anymore. I'm done. I've lost it. I've got to quit,' " she said

But Mark did not quit. He hung in there and worked hard to improve. The hard work paid off. Within two years, he was promoted to the majors. In the big leagues, Mark had a spectacular rookie season. He hammered 49 homers and made the All-Star team in 1987. Not only that but, after the season was over, every single person who voted for the American League Rookie of the Year voted for Mark!

Perhaps the most impressive thing Mark did in 1987, though, was this: He gave up a chance to become the first major league rookie to hit 50 home runs in a season! Why would he do that? Mark skipped the last game of the season so that he could be with his wife during Matt's birth. He already had 49 home runs and might very well have hit another in that game. He didn't care. "I'll have other chances to hit 50 home runs. But I'll never have another chance to see my son being born," Mark said later.

Good Times and Bad

The next three seasons were good for Mark's team. The A's won the American League pennant in 1988, 1989, and 1990. In 1989, they went on to beat the San Francisco Giants in the World Series! Mark continued to slug homer after homer. He smacked 32 in 1988, 33 in 1989, and 39 in 1990. In 1990, he also won his first Gold Glove for outstanding fielding at first base. Mark and Oakland teammate Jose Canseco were called the "Bash Brothers" because of all the home runs they hit.

But all was not well with Mark. His personal life was rocky. He and Kathy were divorced just before the 1988 World Series. Then his professional life got difficult. Over three seasons, Mark's batting average steadily declined, although his number of homers increased. He just wasn't happy with anything anymore. And the fans weren't happy with him! Mark was booed at the ballpark and even taunted by kids who walked by his home in Alamo, California. "McGwire, you stink!" they yelled. Indeed, Mark's hitting was a mess. So he listened to all the people who thought they knew what was wrong. "I must have gotten a hundred suggestions, and I listened to ninety of them," he said. "I can't count how many stances I had . . . or how many bats."

In 1991, Mark again seriously thought about quitting baseball. He batted only .201 and hit just 22 home runs. That ended his streak of seasons in which he'd hit 30 or more homers at four.

Then, one night on a long drive by himself, he did a lot of thinking. He looked closely at his feelings about baseball and life in general. Mark realized that he was depressed and had feelings that he needed help dealing with. He knew he could not fix them himself. He decided to seek professional help. He went to a psychologist. (A psychologist [sigh-CALL-oh-jist] is a person who is trained to help others with their emotions.)

"That was the turning point in my life as a person and as a professional ballplayer," Mark explained later in *Sport* magazine. "Seeking help made me the person I am today. It made me find out what I'm all about. I believe that anyone who confronts his problems succeeds."

By 1992, Mark was back in top form on the ball field. He batted .268, with 42 homers. It looked as if his life were moving forward again.

Unfortunately for Mark, that wasn't the case. Injuries caused him to miss 202 of the A's 276 games during the next two seasons! First, in May 1993, he injured his heel. Then he developed a stiff back. After that, Mark had surgery to repair his heel in late September 1993 and more surgery on the same heel in August 1994. During all these injuries, Mark kept going to the stadium. He studied pitchers and hitters. He worked out to keep in shape as best he could.

Mark was back in 1995, when he hit .274 and 39 homers. Mark accomplished this despite playing only 104 games because of injuries and a long baseball strike.

Mark and Matt

Mark is very close to his son, Matt. They clearly have a great time together. Mark even had a special clause put in his contract with St. Louis that made sure Matt got a seat on the team plane!

"We talk about everything," Mark says. "We talk so much that sometimes we don't even have to use words. We just look at each other and know what the other is thinking."

Their love for each other was obvious when this great slugger lifted his son high into the air after breaking Roger Maris's home-run record. Matt had been waiting for his dad at home plate. It was a moment millions of people remember.

MARK McGWIRE

Mark's body failed him again in 1996, when injuries kept him out of another 32 ball games. He became discouraged. Once more, Mark wondered if he should hang up his spikes forever. But he remembered all that his father had achieved despite the pain he had suffered from polio. That's when Mark put aside his doubts and put himself back onto the field. By the time that season was over, he had belted 52 home runs. He had averaged one homer in about every eight at-bats!

By now, Mark had been nicknamed Big Mac. The next season, he proved that the nickname was a good one: He smashed 58 homers and joined Babe Ruth as the only players to hit 50 or more home runs two seasons in a row. (Since then, Sammy Sosa and Ken Griffey, Jr., have also done it.) He was also picked to be an American League All-Star for the ninth time.

Surprising as it seems, because he was doing so well, Mark was then traded by the A's to the St. Louis Cardinals in July 1997. He was going to be a free agent after the season was over, and the A's weren't sure they could afford to re-sign him. They traded him so that they'd get something in return.

It was a good move for Mark. He loved St. Louis and the people of St. Louis soon loved him. On September 16, 1997, he signed a contract worth at least $30 million and promptly announced that he would give some of that money away! Mark set up a foundation to help abused kids and promised to donate $1 million a year for three years to get it going. Mark broke down in tears when he talked to reporters about his plans. Big Mac is a big man with an even bigger heart!

SUPER 8

The 1998 season earned Mark a permanent place in baseball history. The ball he hit and the bat he used when he smacked his 62nd home run are already in the Baseball Hall of Fame, along with the uniform he was wearing. As soon as he becomes eligible, Mark will almost certainly be elected to the Hall for his outstanding career accomplishments.

A Changed Man

The changes Mark has made inside himself during his career also are impressive. Mark learned that it was not healthy to keep pain and fears locked inside. He learned to talk openly about things and to cry without embarrassment. He had worked to develop a good relationship with his ex-wife and her new husband, who were raising Matt.

Mark arranged his life so that he could spend lots of time with Matt. During the off-season, he lives just five minutes from Matt's home. During the season, Mark lives in St. Louis, and Matt travels to visit his dad often. "Everything I do in life and in baseball now is for my son," Mark says.

On the field, Mark found the strength and will to keep playing baseball, no matter how tough or painful it sometimes was for him. He learned to overcome his doubts and thoughts of quitting and to try harder, instead. That determination enabled him to continue to develop and improve as a ballplayer — and, eventually, to shatter one of the game's oldest and greatest records.

"Mark is incredible," Jose Canseco said in 1998. "No one can stand in his shoes — not Babe Ruth, not anyone. He's in a league of his own."

SUPER 8 SAMMY SOSA

There are more than homers on the mind of this slugger

Home-run madness was in full swing. It was the summer of 1998 and the entire United States, it seemed, was fascinated by the intense, but friendly, home-run race between Mark McGwire of the St. Louis Cardinals and Sammy Sosa of the Chicago Cubs. By late September, both sluggers had passed the long-time, single-season record of 61 homers. They were in new territory, both having hit more home runs than any major league player had ever hit in one year. Only one question remained: Who would finish the season with more homers — Big Mac or Slammin' Sammy? Who would be crowned America's new Home-Run King?

Two men had held that unofficial but very special title for most of the 20th century. The Sultan of Swat, Babe Ruth, had been baseball's Home-Run King from 1919 until 1961. Roger Maris claimed the title in 1961, when he smacked 61 homers. What an achievement it would be for either Sammy or Mark to take over that famous title!

Sammy and Mark were both good sports during their

competition. They joked on television about their rivalry and wished each other well. Still, each player wanted very much to end up as the home-run champ.

As the season drew to a close, the lead changed hands often. Mark would pound a few out of the park, then Sammy would follow. On September 23, Sammy belted two homers to tie Mark, with 65 each. Two days later, both players ripped another one to keep the chase even at 66. This race was going right down to the wire.

Meanwhile, far from the major league ballparks, something terrible happened. A fierce hurricane battered several islands in the Caribbean. One of the islands worst hit was the Dominican Republic, Sammy's home country. Sammy grew up and learned to play baseball in the Dominican. Most of his family and his wife's family lived there still. In fact, Sammy himself still lives there part of each year. Hurricane Georges had destroyed much of Sammy's home country.

Sammy could not put the hurricane victims out of his mind. Many athletes probably would have. They would have focused entirely on being in the greatest home-run race ever. Or they might have focused on the race for the pennant that their team was in. But Sammy couldn't stop worrying about the people in the Dominican Republic. Sammy knew how much suffering a natural disaster like a hurricane could cause.

On September 25, the day he hit his 66th home run, Sammy announced that he was setting up the Sammy Sosa Foundation. The Foundation would make sure to aid his stricken country. After the game on the 26th, Sammy rushed to the Dominican consulate, in Houston. There, Sammy,

SAMMY SOSA

THE SAMMY FILE

BIRTH DATE: November 12, 1968

HEIGHT: 6'

WEIGHT: 210 pounds

BATS: Right

THROWS: Right

FAMILY: Sonia (wife), Keysha (daughter), Kenia (daughter), Sammy (son), Michael (son)

HOMES: Chicago, Illinois and San Pedro de Macoris, Dominican Republic

FAVORITE SPORT TO PLAY (OTHER THAN BASEBALL): Boxing

FAVORITE SPORT TO WATCH (OTHER THAN BASEBALL): Football

FAVORITE ATHLETE: Michael Jordan

BEST FRIEND: Cub infielder Manny Alexander

BEST ADVICE HE EVER RECEIVED: "Do good deeds, and never hurt anyone" — from his mom

along with a couple of other players, helped load supplies and food to be shipped to his country. The home-run chase with Mark was important to Sammy. But helping people in serious trouble receive emergency water, food, and shelter was also important.

Sammy didn't hit a home run on the 26th or on the 27th, when the Cubs played their last regular-season games. He finished the year with 66. Mark hit four in his last two games to end the year with 70 homers! Some people may wonder whether Sammy's worries about the hurricane damage cost him the chance to at least tie Mark's record. No one knows for sure, of course. But we do know that, without Sammy's attention, fewer hurricane victims would have been helped.

So Mark ended up as the homer king. But Sammy did okay, too. He batted .308 and knocked in 158 runs — more than anyone else in the majors. Sammy's great performance also helped the Chicago Cubs make it to the playoffs for the first time since 1989. For his efforts, Sammy was named the National League Most Valuable Player.

The 1998 home-run race also made Sammy famous. All the fans following the race got to see what Sammy and Mark were like. They both became popular across the United States. People learned that Sammy had had humble beginnings and that he was grateful for all baseball had given him. They discovered and came to respect his sense of humor and good sportsmanship. And they admired his efforts to help others, before and after the hurricane.

A Tough Beginning

Long before the hurricane or the home-run race or before Sammy even started playing baseball, it looked as if Sammy didn't have much of a chance to make it big in life. He was just a poor kid from a remote island. No one ever thought he would grow up to become a baseball star.

He was born Samuel Sosa on November 12, 1968, in San Pedro de Macoris, a city in the Dominican Republic. Sammy was one of seven children raised by his mother. His father died when Sammy was just 7 years old. He lived with

SAMMY SOSA

his large family in a two-room section of what had been a public hospital. There was rarely enough food to go around. To help make money, Sammy sold oranges for 10 cents and shined shoes for a quarter on street corners. Sammy also had a speech problem. Kids called him *Gago*, a Spanish word for "stutterer." Life was hard for Sammy.

Sammy liked playing baseball. He just played for fun with poor or homemade equipment. His first glove was made from a milk carton. Rolled-up socks were his "baseball." Most players who make it to the major leagues start learning good baseball techniques when they are very young. Because he was poor, Sammy didn't play any organized ball until he was 14! But just two years after he joined his first team, a major league scout invited Sammy to a tryout!

For the tryout, Sammy had to borrow a uniform, and his shoes had a hole in them. He was a skinny 5' 10" and 150 pounds. He wasn't a fast runner, and he had a wild swing that was too long and loopy.

Still, there were things about Sammy that the scout liked. He was aggressive in the field, and the baseball jumped off his bat. That was enough. The scout signed him to a minor league contract with the Texas Rangers' organization, and Sammy had his big break into professional baseball! The scout gave Sammy a $3,500 contract. That wasn't much by major league standards, but it was a lot more money than Sammy had ever seen.

In 1986, Sammy headed to Florida to play for the Rangers' rookie-league team. Leaving his mother crying at the airport, the teenager flew off to a strange country to start a new and very different life. Sammy didn't speak any English. At first, communicating with teammates and coaches was tough.

"I was lucky because there were some [Spanish-speaking] Puerto Rican players who I hung out with. They helped me a

What's in a Number?

in Sammy's case, quite a lot. Sammy wears number 21 on his Cub uniform. This is in honor of Roberto Clemente, a former star outfielder for the Pittsburgh Pirates who also wore 21. Like Sammy, Roberto was an outstanding player and human being. In 1972, Roberto was delivering supplies to earthquake victims in Nicaragua. The plane Roberto was in crashed, and he died. Roberto was only 38 years old and in the middle of a great career. Roberto's legend lives on. He's a member of the Baseball Hall of Fame. Major league baseball's annual award for the player who best combines outstanding baseball skills with caring for his community is named after him. And Sammy wears his number 21 on his back.

SAMMY SOSA

lot," Sammy recalled. "This is the way I was able to under-stand the life here in the United States."

Sammy's skills needed a lot of polishing. Still, he played well enough to keep moving up through the minor leagues. In 1989, he played in 25 major league games with the Rangers. But Sammy was soon sent back to a Triple A team (the highest level in the minor leagues). Then, on July 29, he was traded to the Chicago White Sox.

Sammy had mixed results with the Sox. In 1990, he was the only American Leaguer to hit 10 or more doubles, triples, homers, and stolen bases. But he also made 13 fielding errors (a lot for an outfielder), struck out 150 times, and batted only .233. In 1991, he batted .203 and hit just 10 homers. Sammy was traded again before the 1992 season began. This time he went across town to the Chicago Cubs.

The move took adjustment because Sammy had never played in the National League. (The Rangers and White Sox are both American League teams.) There were different pitchers and stadiums to get to know. Sammy still had a great deal to learn. "When he first got here [in 1992], you could see he had great physical skills," said Chicago first baseman Mark Grace. "But he was so raw. He didn't know how to play the game."

In 1992, Sammy appeared in only 67 games because of fractures in his right hand and left ankle. But the next season, he began to show his real potential. He banged 33 homers and drove in 93 runs in 1993. He also stole 36 bases to become the first Cub admitted into the so-called "30-30 club." That's a tough "club" to join. You have to have enough power to hit at least 30 homers and enough speed to steal 30 or more bases in one season. It requires a special combination of skills that few players have.

Sammy became the Cubs' regular rightfielder and he posted some impressive numbers over the next four seasons. Among the highlights: He stole 34 bases in 1995, hit 40 home runs in 1996, and knocked in 119 runs in 1997. His batting average climbed as high as .300, in 1994.

But Sammy wasn't consistent. In 1997, he hit only .251. He struck out often, too. That was because he seemed to always be swinging for the fences, as if he thought every hit could be a home run. Sammy also made too many reckless attempts to steal bases. He appeared to be trying to get big statistics for himself instead of working to help his team win ball games.

But there was a reason behind Sammy's behavior. It went back to his poor childhood. It seemed that Sammy thought he needed to steal a lot of bases and hit a lot of home runs in order to keep his job. As a result, he tried too hard to hit a home run or steal a base every chance he had.

That is understandable. Even though he was a wealthy man by 1997, and owned nice houses, drove expensive cars, and gave lots of money to charity, he still had a fear of being poor. And it's not easy to change.

Still, Sammy knew he had to find some way to change his thinking if he really wanted to become a better ballplayer. So, after the 1997 season, he worked with the Cubs' hitting coach Jeff Pentland for the first time. He saw a videotape of himself that showed how rushed and wild his swing was.

SAMMY SOSA

During the winter, he concentrated on hitting to rightfield. He finally developed the patience and poise of a fine hitter. He had become a new man at the plate.

"There was too much pressure last year," Sammy admitted in 1998. "I was trying to hit *two* home runs in *one* at bat. Now I don't feel that [way] anymore."

The difference was soon obvious to everyone. Sammy's bat was ablaze. In June 1998, he broke the major league

A Month for the Record Books

Do you think Slammin' Sammy had a great month in June 1998? No, it was an unbelievable month! He homered in his first and last at-bats and smacked 20 homers, a big-league record for the most homers in one month. But Sammy did more. He drove in 40 runs. He hit 21 homers over the 30-day period from May 25 to June 23. That's the most in any 30-day period in major league history! According to the Elias Sports Bureau, baseball's official keeper of statistics, the previous record had been 20 home runs in 30 days. That mark was set first by Pittsburgh's Ralph Kiner, in 1947, then matched by Roger Maris, in 1961.

home run record for a single month by swatting 20 homers.

Some people develop a big head after so much success. But if anything, Sammy seemed more modest than ever. When reporters and photographers asked Sammy if he would break Roger Maris's homer record, he just talked about Big Mac. "Mark McGwire is the man," he would say. "Maybe tomorrow he'll be motivated . . . and hit two or three [home runs]."

Sammy also seemed to enjoy himself a great deal whenever he was at the ballpark. "Every day a holiday for Sammy Sosa," he would say with a laugh. After Sammy belted a homer, he always kissed two fingers, touched his heart, then blew a kiss. This was a message to his mom, who watched the Cub games on television in the Dominican Republic.

A Good Sport

Sammy's happy style was contagious. It helped make the great home-run race of 1998 a special pleasure to watch. Sammy kept the smile on his face even on the day that Big Mac broke Roger Maris's homer record first. As it happened, Sammy was right there when Mark hit that historic homer. Everyone could see how he handled it. He handled it perfectly! Right after Mark's homer, Sammy trotted in from rightfield and warmly hugged his rival.

"It was a great moment," Sammy said later. "I could see the emotion in Mark's eyes. This is a great moment for baseball and everybody knows that. It's something I'm not going to forget."

He was gracious again in 1999 when the Cardinals and

SAMMY SOSA

the Cubs again ended the season playing each other. Mark and Sammy each hit a homer in the final game. Mark again finished first in home runs, ending the season with 65 homers to Sammy's 63.

"I am a happy man, not disappointed," Sammy said. "I had a great year. For me, that's something to be happy about."

Sammy Claus

Although 1999 was a great year, the 1998 season had been unforgettable for Sammy. He won many honors besides the MVP award. One of the most important was the Roberto Clemente Man of the Year award (see box on page 90). The award was given to Sammy for his charity work, including his aid to the victims of Hurricane Georges. "I'll never forget where I come from," Sammy said months later. "I'm still hungry, and I'm still humble." Sammy is such a generous man that children in his country often call him "Sammy Claus." He delivers presents to kids at Christmas and buys computers for schools.

In July 1999, Hall of Fame pitcher Juan Marichal [MAR-eh-shawl] expressed his feelings during a tribute to Sammy in New York City. His words expressed the feelings of many. "Sammy Sosa, you are a hero to everybody," Juan said, "not only because you play great baseball, but because you are a great human being."

Sammy could hardly ask for a better tribute.

WANT TO HAVE MORE FUN

WITH SPORTS ILLUSTRATED FOR KIDS?

GET A FREE TRIAL ISSUE of SPORTS ILLUSTRATED FOR KIDS magazine. Each monthly issue is jam-packed with awesome athletes, super-sized photos, cool sports facts, comics, games, and jokes!

Ask your mom or dad to call and order your free trial issue today! The phone number is 1-800-732-5080.

PLUG IN TO www.sikids.com. That's the S.I. FOR KIDS website on the Internet. You'll find great games, free fantasy leagues, sports news, trivia quizzes, and more. (Tell your mom or dad to check out www.sportsparents.com, too.)

CHECK OUT S.I. FOR KIDS Weekly in the comic section of many newspapers. It has lots of cool photos, stories, and puzzles from the Number 1 sports magazine for kids!

LOOK FOR more S.I. FOR KIDS books. They make reading **fun!**